Overcoming Your Monsters

By
Lakenya Spikes

About Author

Lakenya grew up in South-Central Los Angeles, residing in her grandmother's house until she could fend for herself. By the ages of 11 and 12, she had matured into an adult who yearned to escape the oppressive environment created by the monsters lurking beneath her grandmother's roof. Fueled by a strong desire for freedom, Lakenya took decisive steps at a remarkably young age to make this dream a reality and wrest control from those who held sway over her.

Recognizing that financial independence was key to her liberation, Lakenya seized the opportunity to work at the age of 13. Her inaugural job was at General Hospital in Boyle Heights, where she earned $5 per hour for eight hours a day. To secure this job, she resorted to forging signatures, knowing her grandmother would not sign the paperwork herself—a bold declaration of independence.

This initial job marked the commencement of a series of opportunities that would shape Lakenya's journey toward the freedom she so desperately sought. Over the course of her life, Lakenya achieved numerous milestones, including becoming an author—an accomplishment that defied the expectations of those who doubted her capabilities. In her pursuit of freedom, Lakenya transformed into someone nobody anticipated she would become, embodying the survival story narrated in the following pages that defines her remarkable life.

Introduction

Hello, beautiful person.

Welcome to the beginning of my ugly truth

With an amazing and beautiful ending

Because God said so! And because I'm a warrior

So, grab your popcorn and relax

Your favorite Author, Ms. Lakenya Spikes.

All the monsters I have encountered in the form of people, situations, circumstances, and decisions that you will soon read about just as you turn the page. These monsters that have come up against me with their personal ugly reflections of themselves that they tried to project onto me could not overcome my light while in my presence. A light I didn't know I had at the time.

The monsters throughout the chapters of this amazing life-changing book still check up on me and are in awe because they didn't stop me from shining. I know the light I carry within me now. I dare those demons to come up against me and the power that I hold in the name of Jesus. They fear me now because of the light I carry and Jesus Christ, who gives me strength.

The hosts that allow those demons to have control of their thoughts, emotions, motives, and behavior that have persecuted, slandered, and betrayed me are not nearly half of the monsters that walk the earth living in the flesh, not in the spirit. They have personal demons that they are not willing to confront and be delivered from. They see no wrong in their evil doings.

The devil will continue to use them for evil, and so will God for good. God sees everything.

My Most Recent Monster

I encountered a monster whom the devil used for wickedness to infringe on my writing skills. God also used her for my betterment to get me started on my writing journey. This particular monster wears a fake smile so well; God exposed her to where only I could see the wicked spirit that lay beneath that fake smile and flattery.

God allowed her to be in my presence for me to learn the things I needed on this writing journey. It cost me $666 and two months of tolerating her fakeness and flattery, with her constantly telling me how amazing my work, chapters, and outline were (which she infringed on)—crazy, right? God also allowed her professionalism to go out the window in my regard. She was supposed to help me professionally accomplish my writing career and help me publish and sell this amazing life-changing book that you will soon read. Instead, she lost me as an amazing client.

I believe God would have done amazing things for her business if she had honestly and professionally helped me accomplish what God wanted in my regard. However, her hidden evil heart, which God allowed me to see, made her do the opposite. God slammed that door shut; her time was up before she knew it. She had served her purpose in my life, and when the time came, I was happy to be rid of her nonsense that only I could see because God was showing me.

Coming into this book writing, God showed me she was like every other monster I had encountered. I laugh now because that monster that was sent gave me confirmation of how amazing and awesome my writing skills really were without knowing she was doing so! I hadn't even gotten started yet. People show their guilt all the time. I know all the signs. No matter how much they try to hide it, God will reveal it. God will give you the eyes to see. Pay attention!

Chapter 01:
Living at 5728

Where I Grew Up

I didn't grow up having role models. I grew up having people I didn't want to be like and seeing situations I never wanted to be in. Living under the roof of 5728 came with embarrassment, slander, hate, evil, disrespect, and discouragement. Not all of us were dealt all aces from a deck of cards, but later in my life, I reshuffled the deck of cards I was given for a better outcome.

Here's my story: As a young girl, I don't remember much about my childhood between the age of 1-5. I really don't remember having any good times as a child at 5728, except for Christmas times when my mom, sisters, and brothers would buy me, my brother, and my little sister (Scarlet) Christmas gifts.

I will say the most memorable memories I do have as a child living at 5728 was making homemade ice cream on the porch by hand and my grandma having her members-only club parties, only because the house would be packed with people drinking and talking loud. We weren't allowed to go to the living room area, but we would sneak and take peeks anyway.

I also remember all my cousins and aunties would come down from Bakersfield to visit, but they were so busy living their lives partying as well as us little people didn't matter. As an adult, I can't tell you the last I've seen any of them up close and personal without the likes of technology in the form of social media.

My 2 uncles lived in that big 3-bedroom house which had an attic and basement. One was one of my mom's older brothers and her baby brother. My mom was the baby girl of my grandma's 6 kids, 3 from one man and 3 from another man. As I grew older, I remember my mom having other babies and leaving them for my grandma to take care of, and my grandma turned around and made taking care of them my responsibility because I was the oldest child of my mom.

It started with my little sister (Miracle) she was born a drug baby; my mom was using drugs while pregnant with her. I remember when Miracle was a baby; she was always crying out of pain when she was picked up; she had to be held a certain way. Miracle's daddy was one of my mom's baby brother's friends, and I didn't like him; my grandma didn't like him either! When my mom was around, he would always come over at nighttime with his radio playing loud music. My mom made me dislike all the men she had dealt with except for (Milton Caves) and (Sir Real); they loved us as if we were their own, and it showed.

To this day, my mom has always put men before her kids. As a child, I was an observer; I paid attention to everything.

Miracle Daddy disappeared before she was even born. By the time Miracle was a year old, she was connected to me by the hip. I was 11 or 12 years old. I could not go outside and play like a regular child unless I took Miracle with me.

How was I supposed to enjoy myself as a child with a child that wasn't mine? I kept Miracle's hair combed, I kept her cute, and I dressed her nicely with clothes other people had given me for her. I love my sister, although my childhood was hindered. I had the responsibility of an adult as a child.

I was combing hair, changing diapers, getting her dressed, feeding her, and protecting her the best way I knew how as an 11- or 12-year-old child. Miracle became my child. My brother and sister were free to be kids and play with their friends. After a while, I became rebellious. I started messing up in school. I became angry in my heart, my thoughts, and my behavior.

I wanted to live free as a child, and I couldn't because of my mom's selfish decisions and my grandma's greed for the county's money. I believe my grandma's thoughts were that as long as she fed us and kept a roof over our heads. That's all she had to do while my mom ran the streets for days at a time.

She would come in and rest up, slaving me around, Lakenya do this, do that, bring me this, bring me that, sending me to people's doors to lie to them for money so when she hit the streets again, she would have money to buy her drugs. These people would ask me questions I couldn't answer before giving me what she told me to ask for. *It was embarrassing*.

I hated when my mom came in off the streets, stanking and bossing me around. I couldn't wait for her to leave again after a couple of days. This was her pattern, and my hate grew more and more for my mom. There were times when I would be out playing with my friends child-free, and here she came all dirty, looking like she hadn't been asleep for days, twitching and grabbing on me to dig in my ear for earwax because she had blisters on her lips.

One time, one of my childhood friend's aunt got mad at what she saw my mom doing to me. She tried to get her to stop, but my mom would not let me go. She kept saying, "This is my child; I can do what I want to her." So, the lady started fighting my mom, and as her child, I defended my mom. I was 13 at the time, fighting a 21-year-old woman because of my mom's selfish decisions.

She was my mom, and I wasn't going to let anybody take advantage of her in her sick state, although I hated her. She always embarrassed me. Long story short, me and my mom formed a back-to-back stance. By the time we formed our stance, my childhood friend's other aunts pulled up, so now it's 3 sisters against me and my mom. In a blackout moment, I just started swinging.

We did what we had to do, and it was over. The next day, while at my childhood friend's house, her aunt came over. She walked up to me with her breast in my face. She was saying things, trying to bully me, but I wasn't scared or had any regrets of the day before. She was mad because one of my punches gave one of her sisters a black eye.

I was upset, though, because, again, my mom had put me in an adult situation. From that day, I was getting into arguments and fights with older women. I had no fear in my heart as a 13-year-old child. I felt like I had to defend myself all the time because of my selfish mom, who didn't have a clue or even care about what I was going through.

There came a time when my mom and I had a fight, all because I wanted to go to my own cousin's wedding, but she would rather my little sister (Scarlet) friend go instead. By this time, my mom had gone to rehab for 12-18 months; she had some drug-free clean time, but so what! I was still angry as her daughter; the anger that had built up in me came out through my words.

On this particular day, I was telling her how I felt, and she couldn't handle the truth. She told me, "I needed to shut my mouth," and of course, I kept talking. She was sitting in her car in the driveway of 5728. I guessed my truth hurt because she got out of her car and came upon the porch where I was standing (no, I was not scared). She tried to close my mouth, and all I knew was that I blacked out with anger and my fist. When I finally came to, we had ended up in my uncle's room on his bed, which is at the back of the house. I was on my back, and she was on top of me with her hands around my throat. I just remember swinging to a point where she could not control me, so she tried to pin my arms under her legs; that didn't happen, so she applied pressure with her hands still around my throat. Eventually, somebody pulled her off me, and I kept saying what I had to say. I still never went to the wedding.

Me and my mom never rekindled that mother-daughter relationship; actually, we never had one from the get-go. I hated her even more. I didn't care if she was clean. My rebelliousness became more unruly and uncontrollable. I was in the office every day at school until I just stopped going. I started ditching; my behavior at home got worse. I started having sex, smoking weed and hanging out with people who I thought were my friends at the time. I felt like nobody loved me at home, so the streets became my home. I stayed in that rebellious state throughout junior high and high school.

In my rebelliousness, I would sneak my boyfriend into my room through the back door while my grandma was sleeping in her room. One night, I got caught; my grandma called me every ungodly name there was except for the one

I was given in front of this man. She, too, lived to embarrass me. By embarrassing me in front of (Nathan Holmes), she actually made him love me. He, himself couldn't understand how someone who is supposed to love you could talk to you like my grandma did me. The next day, he was determined to see me, just to see if I was okay from the words he heard my grandma call me, which would break anybody down. My grandma was something evil to me. He just kept asking me if I was okay. He hugged me tight and deep for a long time. I loved him for caring and not laughing at my embarrassment, which was purposely done.

My grandma always tried to humiliate me any chance she got. The embarrassment was so bad that I was afraid to give my friends my phone number because I knew that when they called and before she allowed me to get on the phone, she would embarrass me, and she did. Sometimes, she would not let me talk to my friends; when I would hear the phone ring that she kept in her room by her bed, I would tiptoe in the hallway up to her bedroom doors and listen. I would hear her say, "Lakenya can't come to the phone right now, or didn't she just leave from where you at? Call her tomorrow." She didn't like any of my childhood friends I had. She wasn't ashamed of letting them know that when they called or even walked to the house to see if I could come outside. When I was allowed to go outside, my friends would say, "Kenya, your grandma mean," and she was evil!

My friends would have sleepovers; I was never allowed to go. The more she said no, the more I became rebellious, to the point that she couldn't handle me. Everybody saw my grandma as this noble saint who took her daughter's kids in. I saw her as this dark, evil woman who hated me. It was as if she was mad at me for having to take care of us. In my heart, I hated her too and didn't know it at the same time; I loved her for not allowing me and my siblings to go into the foster care system. My mom was the same way; she, too, would say some of the most hurtful things. This was after she had gotten clean from drugs; that's why that hate was still there.

The whole time, God had His hands on me, but I didn't know that. It had been many times, I've asked God why did He allow these evil women to be a part of my life? Why wasn't I able to be a child but got pushed into becoming an adult at the age of 13, taking care of kids that weren't mine? Now I understand completely. This book is one of the reasons why. God knew I had to go through everything I have been through to be the person I am today, with tears running down my face as I type these words, having a healed breakthrough moment because now, I understand things I didn't understand back then and why I went through what I went through.

I am not what they have called me. I am not who they tried to say I am. In 2014, my mom called me the weakest link, but God has shown me that I am stronger than all of those monsters who have tried to hurt me. It shows in who I am today! My accomplishments, morals, what I believe in, and all the generational curses I have broken. I feel sorry for all of them because today, I am blessed beyond my measure because of my struggles. Even now, God is with me, still taking care of me as He gives me the edification to give to you through these words as I type them at 4:10 AM. Thank you, Jesus.

Trust that you are not who people say you are. Everything you go through is not meant to hurt you, although it may hurt. Everything is for God's purpose. God has been watching over me my whole life. I have been touched the wrong way in the wrong place by two different men; one of those men is dead! Been dead for many years now, and the other one is still alive with a foot in the grave as I type these words. These are monsters in the form of people.

Being Taken from My Mom

- Where it all started.

I was the chosen one to break the generational curses that tainted my bloodline.

I was taken from my mom by her monstrous sister (Natasha Jordan) and her monstrous daughter (Evelyn Beatrice Kale). I remember in my 2nd-grade year when my brother, my little sister (Scarlet), and I had to go live with them for some reason or another. They lived on 60th Street and Budlong Ave. I went to Budlong Elementary School until my 3rd-grade year. Their house was directly across the street from the school, 2nd house from the corner. The teachers there were hard to get along with because I was in an unfamiliar place starting anew. Over time, I became friends with the other kids on the block a few doors down, who were the children and grandchildren of my aunt's friends. I didn't understand why my brother, little sister, and I were taken from my mom as I do Now! I knew my mom was on drugs, but I didn't know it was that bad that they had to take us from her. We were already living at 5728 in my grandma's house (where my mom resides to this day).

The day we were taken, they all made up excuses that my grandma had to have surgery, which later on I found out she did, but there was something else evil being done. I remember crying and not wanting to go. God showed me years later why we were really taken from my mom. My aunt (Natasha Jordan) hated my mom, her own sister. She hated my mom so much that the hate was passed down to her oldest daughter (Evelyn Beatrice Kale). She and her daughter wanted to hurt my mom in every way possible. The fact that my mom was using drugs made it easier but really had nothing to do with the real reason they took us in. God showed me. It was pure hate that made my aunt take us from my mom; she and her oldest daughter had their own separate motives but worked together. I just told you my aunt's motives; now her oldest daughter, who was also a monster in my life as a child. Her motives were evil on a whole different level mentally. I was her personal sacrifice because her oldest big brother was touching her, and her mom knew and looked the other way; this is why she's blind in one eye today. Stuff like this is a part of why my bloodline was tainted. But this goes all the way back to before I was even born, back in my grandma's younger days. Generational curses are what they are called; anyway, I tell you, not once has my mom been there to protect me. She had never protected me as her daughter. (EBK) oldest big brother stopped touching her and started touching me. God showed me. (EBK) knew every time her monstrous brother came to my bed, which now, I believe, was purposely placed close to his bedroom door. This monster is still alive with a foot in the grave as I type these words. God showed me (EBK) was up every time her monster came to my bed to touch me; God also showed me why throughout the years, as I grew into this beautiful woman who refuses to be a victim, (EBK) would always say I don't like her. Now I know I had reasons not to like her! Most of the time, it was her guilt that kept her saying that. At the start of my spiritual journey, God showed me all of this and more within the circle of my aunt (Natasha Jordan), children, brothers, and sisters sleeping with each other until a child was conceived, which makes him a nephew and a son at the same time. They think nobody knows, but I've been knowing about all their ungodly secrets for years. Ugh! Nothing is hidden from God. Anyway, in 2020, God showed me all these things. God wanted me to forgive (EBK). I didn't want to! Not liking her turned into hate instantly!

God told me He needed me to remove that ungodly anger from my heart that had just come flooding in. I was so angry; my anger turned towards God for showing me what this toxic monster had done to me and then wanted me to forgive her in that same 5-10 minutes. The main reason I was angry was that God wanted me to forgive her! Of course, He let me go through my shock; this was new to me as an adult. He let me get my crying out, which felt like my tears were on fire, burning my face as they rolled down my cheeks. He let me build up anger in my heart for that selfish monster, then turned around and told me He needed me to forgive her, which was a test at the time. I didn't care about the test; I was feeling so many things at that moment. I tell you, if she had been in front of me, the Lord knows what I would have done in that moment.

Anyway, me and God went back and forth with this. I did not want to forgive that wicked person! Here it is; I'm just finding out that this monster put me in harm's way to save herself. I was beyond pissed because I couldn't do anything at the moment but forgive this monster that I felt didn't deserve that from me; it was too early. I was still in shock from finding out that someone who was supposed to love me actually harmed me instead. A rage came over me, yet I couldn't do anything but feel it and go through this process God was taking me through. God was pushing me hard to forgive her, so I finally gave up and said, "I don't know how!" He said, "Go on her Facebook page and heart her profile picture." I tell you, it took everything in me to heart her profile picture, but I did what God told me to do, and immediately, my anger went away. I had stopped crying. I wiped my face. I felt free, and all was good, but I was still hurt, like why? Knowing God had already shown me why.

Then I felt sorry for that monster who had monsters of her own. Isn't that something? To this day, she doesn't even know that the day I hearted her photo was me forgiving her, and if she ever reads this awesome, amazing, life-changing best-selling book, which I'm sure she will because God is going to find a way for it to end up in her hands, she will then know how I felt and that she is forgiven for putting me in harm's way as a child.

The next day, after hearting her photo only because God told me to, she posted another profile picture of her and her husband. I immediately blocked her because I knew she was seeking validation from me. All those years in her head, she believed I didn't like her because of what she knew she had done to me as a child, and carrying that secret around with her was her punishment from God to this day. I can only imagine the help she needs mentally. Living in silence will slowly eat you alive and is actually what the devil wants! Today, I understand that I am no one's enemy, but what's on the inside of them is mine! As a young girl, I do remember (EBK) being insecure about herself a lot. She was a big girl with short hair; she wore glasses, stayed in flip-flops, and cut-off jeans. I believe being molested by her own brother was the cause of this. I've never seen her with a boyfriend. I believe her husband now is the only man she has been with (besides her brother), and she lucked up on him (in my opinion). She had written this rap about herself that went like this:

> My name is (Evelyn E), I'm in the place to be
> I'm the fattest chick in history.
> I weigh 800 pounds, and I can't be beat,
> Listen up, homeboy, this is what I eat.
> I eat 12 loaves of bread, chili beans,
> Hot water cornbread, and collard greens,
> Bacon and eggs and chocolate cake

And I cook my chicken with Shake and Bake,
Liver and onions while I blow my nose
The more I eat, the more it grows.
I can't get any man, you'll soon agree,
My hips are wider than a Mississippi River
But my love is so good it will make you shiver.
I'm a fat girl! LOL.

The first chance she got to cut on or manipulate her body, she did. And she still wasn't happy with herself; she had always tried to look like somebody else from head to toe, except for the person underneath all that makeup. The fake-colored eyes, wigs, and anything else that reminded her of her monstrous childhood household memories, which I'm sure is hard to do. I pray that after all these years, she gets the help she really needs in Jesus' name.

I can't even remember the last time I saw the monster that tried to destroy me as a child, who I have overcome as an adult. The last time I saw my monstrous aunt (NJ) was in in 2018 at my aunt's (Cristy) house for her birthday. (NJ) tried to make me feel some kind of way, playing on her blindness, giving the other family members who were there something to talk about. But God showed me why. Her demons still saw my greatness even then while she was acting like she didn't know who I was because she was pretending she couldn't see me. She was looking at the younger version of my mom again, the one she hated since birth. This generational curse and many others, God has called me to break and speak the truth about, along with mothers hating daughters and sisters hating sisters. I am the chosen one for so many things in my bloodline to be restored.

Yes, I finally told my mom when I was about 31-32 that her nephew was touching me as a child. She wasn't shocked; she wasn't angry. Her response was of one who didn't care. Two months later, the conversation came back up, and my mom told me she had forgiven him without actually doing anything in my defense. It made me feel some kind of way because she had forgiven this monster who touched her daughter without even having so much of a conversation with him.

Three years later, I started my catering business, and because this monster had a hotdog stand/cart, she advised me to go see this monster. I wanted to slap her lips off her face, but I didn't. I didn't want to show her that she had hurt me again with her words by what she had suggested I do. It's like she lives to see me broken down because she is weak. That conversation lit a match that relit the hate I had for her more this time than the first time. The demonic fear people carry within them will have them doing and saying the most hurtful things to those whom they say they love. But like I said before, she has never protected me as her daughter. But God has been watching over me my whole life. I thank God I can laugh now at my mom for still holding resentment in her heart towards me for putting my hands on her all those years ago but has forgiven her monster of a nephew for touching me as a child. I know my mom is jealous of me because my strengths show her weaknesses to this day. God told me to stop fighting for a relationship with my mom because she and my dad's only purpose in life was to bring me into this world for Him so that I could be the supernatural, all-powerful spiritual being I am today through Christ Jesus. God knew what kind of parents they would not be to me, so God took me in and lifted me up (Psalm 27:10).

My Evil Grandma

I never felt the love. I started journaling as an angry teen at the age of 13. I needed an outlet living at 5728, so I started writing down my everyday feelings in a big book of empty pages. I wrote about what I did for the day. I wrote down about who I had sex with or was going to have sex with. I wrote about what the experience felt like and how I felt about it. I wrote down all my private thoughts in this book, which became my personal diary.

I would leave this book on the side of my bed, down on the floor, leaned up against my nightstand when I went outside. The only way you would see this book is if you were on my bed being nosy. Me and my little sister (Scarlet) shared a room; we had old-fashioned wood bunk beds. She had the top; I had the bottom. I had been writing in this book for a while before my book came up missing one day. I looked for this book for days; after about two weeks of my book going missing, on this particular day I was out hanging with my friends. I came in early, and as I walked into the house, I could hear my grandma talking on the phone as I passed her room to get to mine. I saw her with my book in her hands, reading my privacy to whoever was on the other end of that phone; later, I found out it was my aunt (NJ) on the phone.

At that very moment, I felt violated on so many levels. I felt super angry; not only did she steal my book out of my room, but now she was on the phone reading my stuff to her daughter! "You evil witch!" was my thought at the time because that's what she had become to me at that moment—an evil witch. After that, her attitude towards me changed, she was already mean to me but it got worst. I felt the hate daily. I was on punishment all the time. I couldn't go hang out with my friends, which she found a reason not to like. I would ask if I could go out and play, and her response would be, "What do you mean to go out and play?"

I never went outside to hang with my friends; this happened daily as my rebelliousness started to set in on top of everything else I was going through as a teenager who felt unloved by my mom and her evil mother who was taking care of me for her own personal reasons, such as greed, which I knew she was getting a check on the 1st and the 3rd for herself and the 15th of every month.

Anyway, my only thoughts every day were to get my book back. I couldn't sleep until I got my book back.

A few days later, I caught her slipping because she always stayed in her bedroom, where she evidently had my book hidden. I got the chance to go into her room. I had about 20 minutes to find my book. I looked in all her drawers and found nothing. Something told me to look in her closet, and there it was. I took my book and went to my room, writing down all that I was feeling and had been through. Two weeks later, my book disappeared again. This time, I didn't care if she was in her room or not. I walked into her room and went to her closet to get my book, and it wasn't there. This time, it was between her bed and nightstand. I caught her slipping again, but this time, I went through all her stuff. I left papers out of place and drawers opened to let her know I was in her room rummaging through her things. I took my book back, and this time, I hid it in my drawer under my underclothes.

My grandma made me hate her in my heart. Here it is: the people who **we**re supposed to love me were turning me into the monsters they were, and that's what I had become in my thoughts, my behavior, my words, and my attitude. Of course, my grandma made it seem like I was just acting out as a teenager. I am here today to say it was because of how she was treating me in her home behind closed doors, where no one could see who she really was! My sister Miracle is going through the same thing with my mom as I type these words. Everybody outside those walls thought my grandma was a saint just because she was taking care of me, my brother, and my sister (Scarlet). Anyway, cousins of mine would come and get me to try to talk some sense into me. At this time, I had no care to give! My cousin (EBK) would come and get me. I started smoking weed at her house; her husband stayed with the good stuff (I thought at the time, but now I know better). I would steal his weed roaches out of every ashtray I found. This was the start of me becoming super rebellious.

To this day, I journal daily but with positive emotions and positive thoughts, creating my reality in abundance. I am not who my grandma or my mom was sent to make me. The devil lost again!

The moral of this story is…

We all have evil people assigned to us.

Don't let people discourage you; be the best version of yourself that you know how to be.

No matter what is brought up against you, you are made to survive.

"So do not fear, for I am with you; do not be dismayed, for I am your God. I will strengthen you and help you; I will uphold you with my righteous right hand." Isaiah 41:10

Chapter 02:
Grandma Spikes House

Here is where I felt loved, around happy people

On my dad's side were my grandparents, (Dill) and (Billie). They had four children: three sons and a daughter. (A), who is my dad, (T), who is my uncle, (R), who was my favorite uncle, the youngest of the three boys (may he continue to rest in peace), and my aunt (K), who is only 3-4 years older than me. They lived on the west side of town (even now). My Dad's parents always had a lovely, clean home, which I loved visiting as a young girl.

I remember going over there on holidays like Easter, Thanksgiving, and Christmas. My grandfather, rest his soul, was the first one to teach me how to eat sugarcane. I didn't have any friends over there, so it was just me, my little cousin (T. Jr), who I am 10 days older than and my aunt, who is only 3-4 years older than us. I am my grandparents' oldest grandchild at their house, I always ate well. Not that I didn't eat well at 5728, but at the Spikes, there was always a variety of everything. I felt loved. I felt recognized and not overlooked because I was the first and oldest grandchild.

Once I was on the west side at my grandparents' house, I never wanted to come back to 5728 on the east side. To me, it was like day and night, good and evil, sunshine and darkness. After years at this location, my grandparents moved to another place. I made it my mission to be there every weekend.

I remember all my cousins from Compton would come to my grandparents' house. They would play music, party, have drinks, laugh, love, and eat. This was the way family was supposed to be in the eyes of a child. The music they played made me love oldies to this day! I prefer it over all this demonic, brainwashing stuff they call music today! I don't listen to anything else! My grandparents' house was the place to be on Fridays and Saturdays. My uncle (R) was the life of the party; he would dance and pop-lock and was good at it. He was so cool. I loved my uncle (R). Everyone just always seemed happy, and that's what I found myself wanting to be around.

My grandfather used to take us on road trips and fishing trips. I remember going to Salt and Sea, taking road trips to a place where there was nothing but fruit trees of every kind. Both of my grandparents were from back south, Georgia, and Cincinnati, Ohio. They were not afraid to explore the world.

I dreaded Sundays because that meant going back to the real world for me. Every weekend, I was at my grandparents' house. I would call on Wednesday to make sure it was okay for me to come over. My bags were packed Thursday morning, and Friday couldn't come soon enough. My grandfather would pick me up on his way home from work. I would see him make that left turn-off 55th. I would run into the house to get my bags. By the time he drove down and turned around, I was standing in the street, waiting for him to pull up right in front of me so I could get in the car. He drove a black Cutlass with a burgundy interior. Sometimes, he would pull into the driveway, and off I was. My heart was happy primarily to see my grandma Spikes, but mainly to get away from my reality as a child living at 5728.

Being at my grandma Spikes house as a kid was always great; it took me away from my unhappy reality of living at 5728 until it was time to go to bed. I would sleep in the bed with my auntie (K), who is 3-4 years older than me. When she thought everybody was asleep, she would go down on me. As a child I didn't know what was being done. All I knew was that it was something I had never experienced before, and it felt good to me. As a child, I didn't know if it was right or wrong. When she was done, she would ask me to do the same thing to her, when I tried, I didn't like the smell, so I couldn't do what she wanted me to do and she would get angry with me. My aunt is the first and last woman to kiss on my vagina!

As I got older, I started having thoughts about being with women, wondering if what my aunt had turned me onto was the reason why I was having these thoughts. But I knew if I could not go down on a girl back then, I know I could not do it as a growing girl coming into herself. Now that I am a full grown woman, well equipped with wisdom and knowledge. I know that two women together is an abomination to God. As I grew older my aunt and I never became close. I sometimes wondered if what she did to me was the reason? Did she ever wonder if I *still* remembered? If she happens to read my amazing life changing book, which she will. God will find a way for it to end up in her hands. She will find out that I do remember! Like it was yesterday, actually I had forgotten about it, but God brought these memories to the full front just for me to tell my truth. God doesn't forget anything; nothing is unseen by the most high God. Even now, I can't tell you the last time I spoke to my aunt, which is fine with me.

I have endured abuse in the worst way from my own family.

My Favorite Cousin on My Dad's Side

- (J)

As a child, my favorite cousin on my dad's side was (Julie). She was tall and beautiful, possessing a walk that made men crumble. She stayed stylish from head to toe, with her hair always perfectly done. Adorned with rings on every finger and jewelry around her neck, she always kept a car. I never saw her unhappy, not smiling, or angry; her laugh was contagious. I admired her so much that I would sit on my grandparents' porch and just watch her interact with everyone when they came down from Compton. Through the eyes of a child, she was who I wanted to be like.

As I type these words, about two months ago, she called me out of the blue. I was happy to hear from her and told her I was just writing about her in my book, as she called. I could hear her smile through the phone. The last time I saw her up close and personal was at her father's passing, my great uncle, her dad and my grandfather are brothers, making us second cousins.

Our conversation on the phone was shocking, and everything she said, I knew to be the truth, but it was hard to believe what I was hearing because I never saw what she was telling me. I, too, had experienced what she had told me she had faced which made me stop going over to my grandma Spikes house. The fact that my grandma let her unbelieving sisters from back south (whom I had blocked on social media) try to tell her about who I am in Christ Jesus added to my decision. They judged me over the phone with their slanderous conversations, as if God wasn't listening, and My Grandma Spikes stopped calling me. We went from talking every day to, I can't tell you, the last time I spoke to my grandma.

The moral of this story is... We are all different but go through the same thing with different monsters to overcome. Everything that happens to you can either break you or make you stronger. To all who did receive him, to those who believed in his name, he gave the right to become children of God. John 1:12-13.

Chapter 03:
My First Real Love

I didn't anticipate the way he or it would unfold, but it did.

I never anticipated that my first real love would unfold the way it did, but life has its own twists and turns.

It all began when I met a boy who eventually became the father of my children. I was just 11 years old, and he was 13, the brother of one of my childhood friends who is now the aunt of my kids. This boy, with his dark skin and bright white eyes, left-handed, pigtoed, and brave, caught my attention. Despite his intimidating, piercing stare, there was something about him that attracted me. Strangely, I was both scared and drawn to him.

Funny and always able to make me laugh, he became a constant presence in my life as I befriended his sister. Over time, I found myself falling in love with him, although I couldn't quite comprehend what that meant at such a young age. All I knew was that this dark chocolate drop had stirred something in my heart, and in my eyes, he was meant to be mine even before any formal relationship had begun.

There was an undeniable allure about him – those bright white eyes, shiny white teeth, and a beautiful smile that captivated me. It wasn't just his physical features; it was his fearless nature. He seemed unafraid of anything, and his physical prowess, especially his left-handed dominance in a fistfight, signaled a sense of protection that appealed to me. He embodied everything I desired in a boyfriend.

However, reality struck hard as he ended up getting involved with other girls, and to my dismay, they were all friends of his sister. These painful revelations found their way into my journal, a precious possession that often went missing while I lived at 5728.

By the time I turned 13, he was 15, and a significant change had occurred in him. He delved into activities that led him to jail. Our communication took a different form – through writing. It was during this period that I finally had the chance to express my true feelings for him. The love I had for him persisted, and we continued exchanging letters until his release, which happened 15-24 months later.

The boy who went to jail emerged as a grown man. His walk had transformed, no longer pigtoed, and his body displayed a remarkable level of toning from the workouts he engaged in while incarcerated. His skin tone was now silky smooth, and his smile had evolved into something even more beautiful. Confidence radiated from him, and seeing him after all that time only intensified my feelings. My love for the boy had now transformed into a profound love for the man he had become.

Despite his return, he didn't come back to me. I had made a regrettable mistake during his time inside (something I now recognize as unforgivable), likely driven by hurt and a desire for revenge. However, this event prompted a significant change in me. I decided to detach my heart from my sleeve, tucking it securely back into my chest. I made a conscious choice not to allow any other woman to affect me emotionally when it came to a man. This experience marked the beginning of my journey towards becoming a woman unburdened by jealousy – a trait that, to this day, I proudly refrain from, recognizing its potential for causing harm.

In the aftermath of a failed relationship and another stint in jail, our paths crossed again. One day, he called his grandmother's house, and as fate would have it, I happened to be there because his sister had now become my best friend. Our conversation began over the phone, and once more, we found ourselves resorting to written communication. This time, the contents of my heart were more complex, far from the innocent lovey-dovey sentiments of an 11-year-old. I had evolved into a teenager with my own style, confidence, and a newfound sense of self.

Physically, I had developed, embracing my curves, and I exuded my own unique swag and style. No longer reliant on hand-me-downs, I was coming into my own. I styled my own hair, held jobs, and had my own money. My mind was expanding, fueled by a thirst for knowledge, and I was growing intellectually on every level. I had cultivated a new circle of friends on the west side of town, and I was unapologetically becoming me, doing me. Yet, amidst all this transformation, my heart remained tethered to him.

Whenever I learned of his impending release, I would halt everything six months prior to ensure a smooth transition upon his return. This became a recurring pattern until I turned 19 and he was 21. The cycle of him going back and forth to jail persisted. However, this time, when he was released, he came home to me. Having transitioned from a juvenile to a parolee, he underwent the halfway house process. I was officially his woman, and he forgave me for the mistakes of our youth. By this point, I had it all – money, means, and the ability to provide for both of us. I invested in everything he needed to hit the streets in style.

The people at the halfway house were astounded by how well I cared for him. I left no room for anyone else to support him because I had it covered. It elevated his standing among them, garnering respect for both of us – a beautiful, light-skinned woman and a dark chocolate, handsome man. Finally, having him to myself was liberating, free from the worry of competition from other women.

I took care of the details, leaving no more than $60 for him. This act of love drew admiration from those around us, as only a few guys received such care from their loved ones. His first 30 days came with restrictions, no visits or outings, but I visited him every weekend thereafter. Each time, I showed up in style, smelling good, sight and scent that everyone looked forward to, especially him.

Coming from his room and walking towards me, all I saw were teeth, a smile that reflected the joy of freedom. I wore this fly Puma watch on my wrist that caught his attention. He asked for it, and later, he revealed why – he wanted to carry my scent with him all day. The wristband retained the fragrance from the perfume I wore, a tangible connection between us. He ensured nightly phone calls by signing up to use the phone, a cost he could cover with the money I left. I made it a point to always be available for his calls, whether he dialed his grandmother's house or mine.

Finally, he got the opportunity to spend the weekend with his family and me. Most of our time was spent locked in a room at his grandmother's house, immersed in a unique intimacy that encompassed every aspect – physical, emotional, and conversational. It was a side of him I hadn't known before, and the experience deepened my love for him. Back then, he was just a boy mentally, emotionally, and physically. Yet, I now had the man version of him in every sense.

As much as I cherished these moments, the looming return to the program was inevitable. We would be locked in an embrace until the last possible moment before he had to leave. I would accompany whoever was driving him back to the halfway house, savoring the final hugs, kisses, and declarations of love. The program demanded he spend four months improving himself and securing employment before being released to the streets. Failure to meet these requirements meant a return to prison.

During the program, he was allowed to come out during the week to job hunt and work on self-improvement. However, instead of following these guidelines, he chose to spend that time with his family and me. Those stolen moments during the week, limited to two hours each, were filled with joy and fun. We reveled in each other's company, and time seemed to slip away like water through a faucet.

As the pressure mounted with the end of his four-month stay approaching, it became apparent that he hadn't fulfilled the program's requirements. One night, after 8 pm, he knocked on my grandma's door and declared that he wasn't going back, an act considered AWOL. As we sat on my grandma's porch, the phone rang – it was the program looking for him. They questioned me: had I talked to him? Had I seen him? Did I know where he was? In that crucial moment, I made a fateful decision to lie, perhaps fueled by the instinct to protect my man from the police. Little did I know that my lie would unwittingly worsen his situation and, at that very moment, alter the course of my life.

Now, both of us found ourselves on the run; we both knew that they were going to come to my grandma's house the next morning, being that I was his only contact on his paperwork. I was not going to leave my man hanging, so I had to leave my home, my job, everything. He needed me.

We went to Long Beach and lived for a month or so with a friend of his family, who loved him as if he was her nephew. We had no worries at the time. While living there, our daughter was created, but at the time, I didn't know I was pregnant.

Eventually, we had to leave Long Beach, and we ended up in Fullerton, CA, with his mom and baby brother. They welcomed us with open arms; it was something different for me, but he wanted me with him everywhere he went, and I was there. We were in Fullerton for about 3 months, living life and enjoying ourselves, not worried about Los Angeles and what we were running from. In Fullerton, I discovered I was pregnant. I was craving potatoes in any form with extra salt; he was becoming sick every morning, and he started gaining the weight that I was supposed to be gaining.

When I actually got confirmation that I was indeed pregnant, he was excited, happy, and overjoyed at becoming a dad. I believe the news boosted up his sex drive; he just couldn't stay off me – we were like rabbits going at it. He would mark me up with monkey bites all over my body, and I loved it. Back then, being marked in that way was cute.

After some time, we had to leave Fullerton and come back to LA. We ended up in Long Beach again, this time at his sister's house. She made us feel comfortable and gave us our own room. I knew we had to start pulling our own weight because all my funds were almost gone, and we were no longer in Fullerton providing for ourselves as we were. I had not been to the doctor yet, and I was starting to show. When I finally told his sister she was going to be an aunt, she was happy for us. I finally went to the doctor.

I got all my prenatal vitamins, proof of pregnancy, and all the paperwork I needed to be able to apply for county assistance. Thirty days later, I had food stamps and income to help contribute to the house. We were living it up with no worries until one day, a friend of his sister's boyfriend at the time (who is now her husband) - this friend was being chased by the police and led them right to where we were living. He ran through the house and into our room. My wallet with both my and (CT)'s IDs and personal information was in there. The police got my wallet, ran our names, and (CT) was handcuffed because it came back that he was a fugitive. My heart sank deep; by now, I was five months pregnant with our daughter, and it was the first time without him since he first came home to the halfway house. My heart was breaking just seeing him in handcuffs.

In those moments, I became depressed and withdrawn. I stayed in our room for days with his tank top laying on my pillow just to smell his scent until it faded away over time. I would get up to eat and shower, but that's it. A lot of things happened after (CT) left. Eventually, his sister had to move, so we found another place in Long Beach, and we moved in. Things started rocking and rolling in a good way. I still had my own room that I shared with her daughters, which I didn't mind since (CT) wasn't there, and the room was originally her daughter's anyway. As long as I didn't have to go back to 5728 to hear all that my grandma had to say about my situation, she was still evil.

While living in Long Beach, this new housing place by the name of Alpha Properties Management came to the surface. They had a website where you could go to apply for housing, and I did. Eventually, I went back to 5728 to my same old room while waiting for this apartment to come through. By this time, I am huge in the belly and about 8 months along. I always wanted my own house, so with some of the money from my paychecks I was getting from the jobs I had before I went on the run, I had already started purchasing things for my own house without having one yet.

I bought my kitchen and bathroom stuff and kept it all in these 2 big blue barrels I had in my closet that my grandma knew nothing about. When I did move, I already had everything for my kitchen and bathroom that I needed. Lo and behold, Alpha Properties Management called me to come in and sign paperwork and to receive my keys for a place; it was single, and I took it. It was just me and my soon-to-be-born daughter anyway, so why not? Plus, her dad would have a place of his own to call home.

I moved into my very first apartment on 12/13/1997 - what a wonderful Christmas present. I had everything I needed for my new place except for a bed, and the crazy thing is my mom bought me a queen-size bed and said, "It was a Christmas present." It was right on time. God was showing me his hand, but at the time, I couldn't see it because I was living in the world. Thank you, Jesus.

By the time I had my daughter, I had my own place. I had income. God made sure I needed nothing to start this new journey of becoming a mother by myself. My daughter was born 45 days later after I had moved into my own place. She was actually due on her dad's birthday, but I had her 10 days later. I was 41 weeks pregnant; I still had my mucus plug, and I had not dilated, not even one centimeter. They had to induce my labor because she didn't want to come out.

(CT) called while I was in the hospital in labor at this time. The contractions I was having would not allow me to talk to him; I actually threw the phone; I was in so much pain. I was trying not to get that epidural. When I tell you, I held out for as long as I could (which probably explains why

I now have a high tolerance for pain), lol. After so many hours of trying to stand my ground, I got the epidural; lol, the pain became unbearable, and I couldn't take it anymore. I was in labor from Monday afternoon to Wednesday morning, going through this all by myself. I was scared. I had no support system. No one called and checked up on me.

Thank God I had nurses that were assigned to me, and they were awesome. They took great care of me in every way; they were very encouraging, which made things easier. I was relaxed after receiving the epidural that I did not want. Wednesday morning at about 5:00 am, the doctor stopped the epidural medicine because it was time for me to start pushing. I began pushing at 6:00 am on the dot.

I went through the pushing process for 3 hours because my baby just wanted to stay in the womb. About 10 minutes before she actually came out, (CT)'s mom and sister walked into my room, and all I could do was cry and push at the same time. They both saw her being born; that was the first time I did not care about another woman seeing me down there, lol. I was exhausted from pushing; my nurse showed me how to use my muscles to push so that I would not get split by my daughter's head. I did not need stitches. Thank God! Everything is naturally still intact how it's supposed to be.

From the hospital, I went back to 5728, back to my old room, because I needed help with my newborn baby. As a new mother, I did not know what I was doing and didn't want to be alone. My mom stayed around the corner with my baby sister's dad (oh yeah, it's 6 of us by this time), and by this time, my mom had been clean for a few years now, and our mom-daughter situation was still the same. I hated her a lot less, though, but the hate was still there. I was happy that she was finally clean because she had been in and out of rehab, doing 15-18 months each time for years.

I was thinking maybe she could be the grandmother to my child that she wasn't the mother to me (hopefully). The funny thing, though, was that she actually told me to get rid of my baby when she found out I was pregnant, and I told her no!

She then asked me, "Who was going to take care of my baby?" and I told her, "I was!"

I guess she thought I was going to follow in her footsteps with my children. That was a cycle I was determined to break! And I did! I have 2 children, a daughter and a son, by the same man, whom I raised with little to no help, and they are both grown now, one 25 and the other will be 21 in a few months as I type these words.

Anyway, while I was at 5728, I knew my grandma still felt some type of way about me, and I did not care. She couldn't tell me anything; I was grown and vowed to take care of my baby by myself no matter what. After being at 5728 for about a week, I needed some air. One night, I fed, changed, and put my daughter to sleep before stepping outside on the porch. I'm not sure how long I was out there, but when I opened the door to come back in, I could hear my daughter screaming at the top of her lungs from the back of the house; she had to have been crying for a while.

I rushed to my baby, thinking she had fallen off the bed or something. As I passed by my grandma's room, she was just sitting on her bed, doing her word search puzzle book, listening to my baby screaming. Evil witch was my thoughts again. I was pissed, but I knew then it was time for me to go to my own new home and start this long journey alone or until (CT) came home.

The next day, I went home and was glad I did. Thank you, Jesus. I got my phone hooked up. I gave (CT)'s family my number just in case he called, and he did. That first call was for the rest of our lives. (So, I thought).

By this time (CT) was in Chino, he had already seen my daughter when she was just 11 days old. Yes, I took her to visit her dad, and he was overjoyed when he saw his twin. Thanks to his grandmother's husband, who was willing to drive us out there every other weekend. Of course, I had to buy gas, which I didn't mind. Witnessing my daughter with her dad was worth everything. I saw another emotional side of him, and she looked just like him; he couldn't deny her if he wanted to. I think him looking at himself through her eyes blew his mind. (CT) was released a week before our daughter's first birthday. He surprised me because I didn't know he was coming home.

On this particular day, his sister was watching my daughter while I went to work. When I got off work and went to pick up my baby, they were both gone. Nobody would tell me where they were or where they went. Hours passed by, and I was still waiting for them to pull up. When they finally did, (CT) got out of the car smiling. I'm smiling, just reminiscing on that day; I can still see his teeth as I type these words. The joy I felt in that moment is indescribable, and the fact that we, as a family, had our own place. I know for sure he was happy to be free, and everything seemed to be falling into place. (So, I thought.) Don't get me wrong; things were good for a while.

Eventually, the streets got the better of (CT) after his release. They released him on parole, and he had to drug test and better himself in some way. Every time (CT) went for a drug test, it came back positive for THC to the point of a violation. He had to turn himself in, and heartbreak struck again—six months or more. He turned himself in, and we were back to our pattern, this time as adults and with a child. He went and served his time, and I kept working. Only allowed my little sister, Scarlet (she's 18 by this time), to watch my daughter (Crystal Stairs was paying her for me). Until they did, we agreed that I would pay her every week, and when she received her fat check, she would give me back what I had given her, and that's what we did.

As I type these words, I can see clearly that God has always had his hands on me. (CT) came home, and I got pregnant with my son (CTJ). Not immediately, but this is when things started changing for the worst.

My Favorite Cousin On My Mom's Side

(DH) holds a special place in my heart as my first real love. Describing this beautiful person is a challenge because there are so many aspects to appreciate. I can confidently say that she loved me with her whole heart, unconditionally. In her eyes, I could do no wrong, and she never passed judgment on me. Similarly, I held no judgment for her; her heart was truly extraordinary. She shared a trait with me as a people pleaser, and I had to learn that God's approval was the only one that truly mattered.

(DH) was a constant source of positivity. She wore a perpetual smile, laughed freely, and had a unique ability to make others feel good, even when she had her own troubles. She entrusted me with many family secrets, which were later confirmed by God. These are secrets known by my aunts and older cousins. My love for her was so profound that it even caused some tension with other cousins. She was an integral part of my life, and I was willing to go to great lengths for her, including bearing a child for her since she couldn't have one of her own. Although we never completed the paperwork or went through the process, we frequently discussed the possibility. Consequently, I allowed her to raise my son during his first year, and I must say she did an exceptional job.

When I picked him up on Fridays, he had already been well taken care of; she made sure he was well-fed and happy. She was the only person I trusted implicitly with my son. There were no unexplained bruises, and she went above and beyond to protect him, ensuring all his needs were met. Her love for my son was akin to a mother's love. She possessed qualities that would have made her an excellent mother, just as she was an outstanding aunt, cousin, friend, and confidant.

As I pen down my thoughts about her, the ache of her absence is palpable. She was the only one who consistently cheered me on in all my positive endeavors. Her encouragement was unwavering; she wanted nothing more than for me to succeed in everything I pursued. She was the only one who truly understood me, a realization that only became clear when God revealed it to me that we are one in the same. Her spiritual calling aligned with what God intended for her, particularly in breaking our generational curses. Unfortunately, she missed her calling in this regard, and the torch was passed down to me.

I stand firm, ten toes down, actively breaking the generational curses that have tainted my family's bloodline. The later chapters of this compelling and life-changing book will delve into the profound impact of this journey.

Pulling up to her house, regardless of its location, was always a special moment for me. Before I could even step out of the car, whether I was within the gates or on the porch, her voice would ring out, hollering, "Poooooh" – her personal nickname for me, a name reserved exclusively for her use. She had a way of making me feel uniquely loved and cherished.

Her habit of leaving encouraging voicemails, accompanied by her distinct laugh, created memories that linger in my mind. As I type these words, I wish I could hear that laughter up close and personal, reliving those moments and trying to hold back tears that threaten to blur my vision. The tight bond we shared became glaringly apparent only after she passed away eight years ago. However, even before her departure, I sensed there was something exceptionally special between us.

The five years following her passing were incredibly challenging for me. Every November, a gloomy cloud seemed to settle over me, making it a particularly difficult month to navigate. It took me about three years to realize that I hadn't truly let her go. Then, in a divine act, God allowed her to visit me in a dream.

In this dream, I was getting married, and she played a pivotal role in making my day extraordinary. The setting was a bright white room adorned with red hearts everywhere. It was just the two of us, and she took charge of everything – from my hair to purchasing my dress. She did it all with a constant smile on her face. When she finished styling my hair, she turned me toward a mirror, and I remember hearing myself say, "I'm so beautiful." That dream, meticulously recorded in detail upon waking, became the last time I saw (DH)'s face and heard her laughter as if she were present in the here and now.

This dream carried a profound message, assuring me that someday I would get married and everything would be taken care of. I eagerly await for God to manifest this dream into reality. In that dream, I felt as though she was telling me it was okay to let her go, with the promise that we would meet again. And so, I did.

Since that dream, every November has been marked by miracles in my life, with blessings coming abundantly. It was in November 2022 that I began writing this incredible, life-changing book, and now it is in your hands as the reader. I encourage you to embrace the miracles it brings and enjoy the transformative journey it unfolds.

(DH) stood as the black sheep of our family, much like I find myself amidst the entire extended family. She faced judgment from my older cousins, just as I do from the broader family. Her existence was marked by being spoken about in hushed tones and looked down upon, especially by her immediate family members, such as her sisters, who deemed themselves superior simply because they didn't follow in her unconventional footsteps. (DH) was a free spirit who embraced her unique way of life. Despite the judgment and criticism, she remained a shining light in the room, much like myself. There was always darkness attempting to dim her light, but in my eyes, God allowed her to shine because we shared a kindred spirit.

As the years passed and I underwent spiritual training, I came to understand that (DH) may not have received the love she truly deserved from those around her, which is why God called her to be with Him. I recognized that my love alone couldn't have filled the void left by the lack of genuine love in her life. Even now, I believe she watches over me, cheering me on with words like, "Go Pooh, go Pooh, go Pooh." It wouldn't surprise me if God assigned her to be one of my guardian angels, silently guiding and protecting me in ways I may not even be aware of.

The moral of this story is simple yet profound – love purely. (DH)'s story serves as a reminder that genuine, unconditional love has the power to uplift, heal, and bring light to even the darkest corners. In a world often clouded by judgment and misunderstanding, embracing pure love allows us to break through barriers, creating connections that withstand the test of time and adversity. So, in every interaction and relationship, let love be the guiding force, transcending judgments and fostering a deeper understanding of the unique journey each individual undertakes.

Chapter 04:
Wanting My Own Everything

Before I could buy anything, I had to resort to stealing. MY EVIL GRANDMA, despite being strict, ensured we had three meals a day, clothes, and attended school. Unlike my friends, I never had money. My grandma didn't believe in giving allowances. She only gave me $1.50 a day, always in coins, during junior high. I had to save it from Monday to Thursday for a little extra on Friday. On the 1st and 15th, she'd give me $5 when her checks came, leaving me to decide between saving it for school or buying dinner that day. I often opted for two hardshell tacos from the hamburger stand on Compton Ave and 55th, which cost $1.25 at the time. Whatever remained, I'd either use at school or keep in my pocket to add to the $1.50's on school days.

My grandma's frugality contrasted sharply with my friends' parents, who gave them $100-$150. It was embarrassing not to have money. Though my friends bought me things, I wanted to buy my own. So, at 13, I began secretly applying for summer jobs my grandma didn't know about. I forged her signature on the paperwork, knowing she'd refuse if asked. Providing for myself meant she would lose total control over me.

As a teenager, my grandma wasn't providing me with what I needed. When I asked for things, she'd question why, but as a woman, she knew why. I didn't feel the need to explain, so I started stealing everything a teenager needs for hygiene. Over time, my 4-foot dresser was packed with lotions, deodorants, hair products, pads, tampons, and more. I didn't need anything for months; I had stolen so much. When my grandma started asking questions, I lied until I couldn't anymore.

By then, I had everything I needed as I grew into myself. With my mom absent and my grandma too mean to teach me, I had to learn hygiene on my own. My first summer job was at General Hospital with (CT) sister who was my best friend at the time and is now my children's aunt. We worked in admitting, earning the minimum wage of $5 an hour. I loved it because I was earning my own money to buy what I needed. Every summer until I turned 21, I made sure to have a job, gaining valuable experience in different places each year. That's why my resume is so impressive today, and I always get the jobs I apply for. I have kept all my check stubs from over the years, though the numbers may be hard to read. By age 17, I was fully taking care of myself.

I was so focused on self-care that my grandma became my bank, holding onto the money I gave her from every paycheck. By then, I was barely living at 5728. My younger siblings had grown up and were finding themselves while I had blossomed into a beautiful butterfly. With the perfect body, tattoos accentuating my features, flawless skin, and naturally long, pretty hair reflecting my personality. Every item of clothing I purchased fit perfectly, and I never wore the same thing twice; if I did, it was months apart. I was unstoppable, enjoying life with my new found friends, until I introduced (Delilah).

Delilah, older than us and a mother, was someone I'd known for a long time, she became another monster in my life. Let me rewind to when I was a child living at 5728, after my siblings and I were taken from our mom. It felt like an eternity before we returned to my grandma's house, where she was recovering from stomach surgery before she could care for us again. During our absence, my mom's younger brother had a girlfriend named Delilah, nicknamed Adidas. She was 16, he was 21. Despite my grandma's initial dislike, she tolerated Delilah as she tried to fit in. Over time, she earned acceptance by caring for my sister Scarlet's and my hair, even braiding it with beads, transforming us into different, but welcomed, little girls.

About a year later, Delilah became pregnant, leading her to stay with us permanently instead of just spending the night. Her baby, my little cousin, was born, and as the years passed, Delilah's demeanor shifted from kind to mean and angry. Her strained relationship with her mother and my uncle's infidelity with woman nearby contributed to this change. Despite my uncle's attractive qualities, including his light skin and flashy Cadillac, his cheating led to more turmoil. Despite the difficulties, they had another child while still living in my grandma's house, occupying his bedroom. Eventually, they moved to Westco, and though we missed them, we cherished our visits, where we could enjoy good food, swimming, and freedom from constant negativity. Delilah would always ensure my sister and I had our hair done during these visits, a treat that lasted until the next visit. After some years away, they returned to the neighborhood.

By then, I was around 15-16 years old, with a curvy figure and long, beautiful hair that I styled as I pleased. Delilah took me under her wing, and despite our age difference, we became inseparable, growing together as best friends. I witnessed the abuse, arguments, and control dynamics between Delilah and my uncle.

As a grown woman, she had to seek permission for specific activities, places, and even clothing choices, while I embraced becoming my own person, discovering my talents, creativity, and voice with the firm belief that no one would control me. My respect for my uncle dwindled. I witnessed Delilah, who I spent a lot of time with, cheat on him. She would give me the car for a few hours while she did her thing.

Despite knowing all her secrets, I never betrayed her by exposing them. I endured her adult attempts to slander and persecute me out of jealousy and envy. No one can question my loyalty! I still keep people's secrets, even those I no longer associate with, despite being betrayed in the worst way. This is why I consider myself blessed; my heart remains pure.

During the abuser's work hours and her boys being at school, she had until 4:30 pm every day to do as she pleased, and I was there with her. On a particular day, we went to get our nails done. I designed my long, super-curved nails in red, white, and black, playing with my creativity. When we showed our nails to my uncle upon returning home, he preferred my design. Delilah instantly got upset and, after calming down, confessed her jealousy towards me and explained why.

At the time, her words went over my head, but in hindsight, she was telling the truth. From that day on, she began covertly competing with me (which I didn't realize then), but looking back over time, her jealousy had morphed into envy. Whatever I did, she tried to do it too, but she always went overboard. She constantly sought to outdo me or copy ideas I came up with. For example, when I started collecting keychains, she did the same. If I bought a small world-design tote bag, she got a bigger one. Even with my hamster and its small cage, she went and bought a whole family of hamsters with a large, elaborate house. Back then, I was oblivious to all of this. I was blind to how she truly felt about me.

Her jealousy escalated because my breasts and booty were bigger than hers, and I looked good in anything I wore. I had the freedom to do as I pleased without seeking permission, which she envied. She wanted the same freedom but was tied down by a controlling man, his insecurities, and two sons. I introduced her to my friends, and eventually, she tried to turn them against me. Years later, she attempted to turn my own sisters against me because she envied the close relationship I had with my sisters. To this day, they still tolerate her, but I don't deal with fake people. It took me 20 years to realize that this person, who envied me, was actually my enemy because my creativity led my uncle to prefer my nails over hers all those years ago.

Reflecting on the hurt caused by this person who pretended to love me, I can't help but feel sorry for her. She needed someone to unload her anger on, and unfortunately, I was there as a friend, a support system. I was the light in her life, but she couldn't see it amidst her darkness. People often project onto others what has been done to them. But God said, "Enough is enough."

Once again when I launched my loaded fruit jar business in 2014, she and her adult son attempted to claim the idea as their own. While I advertised my product on social media with words and photos, she stole my pictures from social media, shared them in secret groups, and pretended they were hers. When she confessed her actions to me, I decided to patent my product and its ingredients, allowing me to take legal action against anyone who copied my idea. I publicly shared proof of my product's patent on social media, to which she responded with surprise. Yes, I took that step to protect my creation. Witnessing her jealousy and envy firsthand made me realize I couldn't trust her with anything of mine. I prayed for guidance, and God closed the door between us firmly.

Even now, she visits my Facebook profile to check on my activities, keeping her envy alive, but she gets blocked every time. Since writing my transformative book, which remains unknown to most, I've had to block her. I find humor in how the devil used her actions against me, yet God turned it into a blessing by removing her from my life. I thank Jesus for that! There's much more I could say about her, but I've grown tired of writing about her. While I've forgiven her, it doesn't mean I have to engage with her. To me, she remains a negative presence. I find satisfaction in portraying her as a character in my book. As it's written, the wicked shall fall in Jesus' name. Some fail to understand that what God has destined for you is yours alone; others attempting to claim your ideas and creativity as their own will never succeed because it wasn't meant for them in the first place.

The lesson here is that it's okay to feel angry sometimes, but don't let it drive you towards revenge. Express your anger, but don't let it consume you or linger. Remember not to give the devil too much power over you (Ephesians 4:26–27).

You deserve what God has in store for you. No one can take that away from you because it's a gift meant specifically for you. Those who try to steal your creativity or ideas lack imagination and confidence in themselves. They don't have the same dreams and aspirations as you.

Chapter 05:
Becoming free to be me

Westside Friends: Growing Together and Apart

As I came into my own, still rebellious yet respectful, I embraced the freedom to live life to the fullest. Among these new companions, we formed a close-knit group of self-motivated young women. We were called Flava! Each of us had a unique nickname like cherry, apple, raspberry, black cherry, skittles, strawberry, peaches, kiwi, grapes, brown sugar, brownie, caramel, vanilla, pina colada, and more. They became my family, and together, we partied from Sunday to Monday while juggling work and school.

Apple, one of the crew members, doubled as our hairstylist, skillfully tending to all our hair needs. Our bond was unbreakable, and we were selective about who we let into our circle. We kept our gatherings exclusive, partying amongst ourselves and forming a vibrant community of individuals. Each day brought new and exciting adventures with us.

Our hangout spot started at Strawberry's house, located off Jefferson and 5th Ave on the west side, which I deemed the best side due to its cleanliness and the kindness of its residents. Strawberry's mom was exceptionally laid-back, often allowing us to spend the night and attend school from her place. Some of us would return home to shower before meeting up again at school to repeat the cycle. As I've mentioned before, I was hardly ever at 5728.

Among our group, drinking was common, but only myself, Strawberry, and Peaches indulged in smoking. We were confident, vibrant, financially comfortable, and brimming with life. Reflecting on these memories brings a smile to my face; we were a force to be reckoned with!

Every time we walked down the street, someone would try to holler at us. Whatever we did, we did it together. We all adored Strawberry's mom and enjoyed going to her house until Strawberry had to move away. She gradually faded from the group, but that didn't stop us from hanging out. Soon, (a)'s house became the go-to spot, and that's when Flava began to flourish. (a)'s mom was amazing too. Every summer I spent with them, we all kept busy with work. I was living so freely at that time that thoughts of 5728 were far from my mind until I needed to visit the bank.

We spent our time at the nail shop and the Saluson Swapmeet. Fantasy Nails on Florence and Fig was our spot. Each day brought a new outfit because every night, something exciting was happening. We always attracted attention wherever we went. Since none of us had a car, we either walked or took the bus until Blackcherry got her BMW. Life became even more exciting, and we enjoyed our youth to the fullest, frequenting 18+ clubs. However, things changed when brownsugar (Delilah) joined the crew.

We all worked at Cherry Communication off Wilshire and Normandie. We'd meet at a designated bus stop and ride in together until Kiwi got her little red Honda. We used to squeeze into that car, sitting on laps. Our stint at Cherry Communication didn't last long. Despite being in an office together on the 5th floor, trying to sell the service they offered, we weren't discouraged until we realized it was commission-based and none of us were making sales. That put an end to it quickly.

Some days, we'd visit Kiwi's house, which I think was in Boyle Heights. I'm not entirely sure; all I remember is driving up hills and making sharp turns until we reached her place. Her mom was really cool; she'd cook sticky rice and some delicious chicken that didn't quite look like chicken, but it tasted amazing. To this day, sticky rice is all I eat. Did I mention Kiwi is Cambodian?

From Kiwi's place, we'd often head to (a)'s house; her room was always filled with us. She had a huge king-size bed where we could all squeeze in. Since her mom was usually at her grandma's house, we practically had the place to ourselves. We'd hang out on Hoover between 73rd and 74th, sometimes we'd get dressed and chill outside. It seemed like the guys were always waiting for us to show up, even our male friends who later became part of the crew, they were all good-looking. Even (A's) brother and his male friends started joining us at her place or in his neighborhood. We were drawing attention because we were new faces on the scene. Their local girls didn't really like us, but they tolerated us because we were friends of (A) plus her family lived on that block.

In 2018, I began developing and testing my hair growth formula. I tried it on myself for 18 months, and within two months, I noticed significant improvements in length and thickness, so I kept using it. I wore my hair in a bun during this time, and after 18 months, I realized it had grown at least four times longer, if not more. I was eager to see the results of my effective formula. Let me share the whole story with you. In 2019, I reached out to someone I considered both a friend and a longtime hairdresser (A) to have my hair pressed and see the 18-month-long-awaited growth results.

The person who had been styling my hair for over 15 years had prevented me from appreciating my remarkable hair growth by cutting it off out of jealousy and spite. Despite my daughter initially doubting my claim that my envious wig-wearing friend had cut more than just my split ends, so again in 2019, I began the process anew. Fifteen months later, my hair had grown four times its previous length, even without being pressed.

However, let's go back in time. My former hairdresser had been hospitalized a few years before the incident where she cut my hair. Looking back, I know my prayers played a role in her recovery from what the doctors deemed a near-death situation. They marveled at her survival, saying she "should have been dead when she got to the hospital" and questioned how she even made it there. A couple of years later, she had experienced hair loss due to medication, which, in hindsight, I believe happened for a purpose known to God. Despite her actions, my prayers played a part in her healing.

One of our last conversations was her telling me she still sleeps with the cross under her pillow that I gave her during her hospital stay. Interestingly, one morning, her and her jealous cousin (KB) had a conversation about me, unaware that I was privy to their discussion. Her cousin harbored envy towards me as well.

I don't miss any of them as time has passed. They never showed up for anything I had going on anyway, which was God's way of revealing their true colors - they were never my friends, just fake supporters who didn't truly support me. Despite their absence, I continued doing my thing without them. God has a way of revealing people's true intentions. I can only imagine the envy in their hearts when I started pursuing my passion for nails, pretending to support me while secretly wishing for my failure. You can judge people by their actions, not their smiles or words. Those who pretend to support you but work against you are eventually exposed by God. I'm grateful to be free of them. As I've said before, "people change." Besides writing about these fake friends, I haven't thought about them again. They're all facing their own struggles in some way.

It's not a miracle to make a hundred friends; the real miracle is finding a single friend who stands by you when hundreds are against you. Cherish friends who genuinely care for you and want the best for you without any ulterior motives. Shoutout to low-maintenance friends - the ones you may not talk to for months because life keeps you busy, but when you do meet, there's nothing but genuine love. True friends are happy for your successes, even if they're going through tough times themselves. When you're doing well, they're happy for you because they understand that your success is their success too.

Be cautious when following the masses; sometimes, the "m" is silent. A friend who stays silent while someone slanders you is also your enemy. A friend turned foe has likely harbored hate from the start.

To all those who pretended to be my friend, it's all fun and parties until you wake up decades later with no savings, investments, qualifications, or job—just a collection of pictures and memories of people you no longer talk to. When true colors emerge, be grateful, as now you know their true selves. Keep your circle productive and practice self-discipline.

The moral of the story: You may be friends for decades, only to realize they were never true friends. I've witnessed this firsthand. You can't conceal the ugliness in your heart; it will be exposed. Be mindful of who you consider friends.

Chapter 06:
Being the Mother that I Needed

My first apartment, responsibilities, and raising a child

When I tell you, I was so happy to have my own place, I mean it. I felt beyond overjoyed. Having my own rules and keys meant no one could tell me what to do. Most of all, I was thrilled because when (CT) came home, we had our own space, our own family. I took great care of my place, always cleaning, even if it wasn't dirty. I just appreciated having my own house.

I was in the perfect location. The bank was next door, the gas station was across the street on the northeast corner, the metro redline was on the northwest corner, and the grocery store was just 2 blocks away. I had the choice of Vons or Ralphs. Everything I needed was within reach, and I got to spend quality time with my daughter.

After my 6th-week checkup, I went back to work, and only my little sister, [Scarlet], was allowed to watch my daughter. I didn't trust anyone else with her (experiencing family to be the first to hurt you). I paid her $50 a week until Crystal Stairs kicked in, which took months. But when they did, my little sis was happy to return everything I had given her, and she was still doing well.

Sometimes on the weekend, my little sis and her friends would come over, hang out, eat, and then leave, which I enjoyed. Having my own place allowed me to be comfortable by myself. I had my daughter, so I wasn't truly alone—she's my everything. Sometimes I'd visit family, but only if I was being picked up and dropped off, which was rare because nobody wanted to drive all the way to my house. I didn't take my daughter on the bus at all in her first year—I didn't want her exposed to germs or anything!

Anyway, I did everything I could to protect my daughter by all means, which is probably why to this day, 25 years later, she turns to me for everything, including prayer. Her dad came home 10 days before her 1st birthday. He was happy to have somewhere to call his own, with privacy. I was happy that he was home, considering he had been gone since I was 5 months pregnant. The loneliness was gone. I had my man. One thing about (CT), he never cheated on me, but there was a line of women waiting for us to break up.

We were living well. Rent was $75-$100 a month. I kept a job and always took care of (CT). Eventually, I grew tired of doing that because I felt like I was sacrificing myself to provide for my family. I had to ask myself, who was taking care of me? The answer was nobody.

As time went on, I got pregnant with my son, who is now 20 as I write this amazing, life-changing book. During my pregnancy with him, I worked until I couldn't anymore. I went through a few changes that I didn't experience with my daughter. First, when I got pregnant, I knew he was my son. To prove myself right, I didn't get an ultrasound until I was about 8 months along. The doctor confirmed what I had already known.

My hair grew so much, I kept it in three braids. My feet were so swollen that I couldn't wear tennis shoes. I stayed in sweats and house shoes; my skin was so pretty. I was all belly and butt, like Yoshi the dragon, but I felt beautiful. My baby boy enhanced me in so many ways. By this time, my daughter was 4 and had experience riding the redline metro train, which was much cleaner than the bus.

We traveled to the east side of town to (CT)'s grandmother's house via metro. If I wanted to visit my family, all I had to do was walk around the corner, though that was rare. (CT) would go hang out with his friends while I would spend time at 5512 with his family, whom I considered mine as well. I allowed his family to enjoy spending time with my daughter.

(CT) and his grandmother had a special bond, and she also shared a special connection with my daughter. I enjoyed seeing her hold my daughter. The way she held her spoke volumes without saying a word. My daughter looks just like all of them—from (CT) to his mom, his grandmother, and his sister. She looks nothing like me; she doesn't even have my skin color. Only now, when she styles her hair a certain way, can I see myself in her. She does have my lips; I shaped them on her face by wearing lip liner while I was pregnant.

As she grew older, we didn't allow anyone else to discipline our daughter, which upset (CT)'s family. We were the only ones who disciplined her, and we were told to keep her at home if she couldn't be disciplined by anyone other than her parents. My daughter wasn't a bad child; her dad's firmness was enough to correct her behavior.

My son was born in August 2002. The day I brought him home, things started going downhill with (CT). After my 6th-week checkup, I returned to work, and this time, their dad was home to watch them. However, he began to change into someone I didn't recognize. He started staying out all night, coming home at 5:00 am or 5:30 am, just as I was leaving for work. When I returned from work, he would be dressed and ready to go out with his friends.

One morning, he came home extremely intoxicated, his eyes dilated, and he had a strange odor on him. It wasn't marijuana—it turned out he had been using PCP. I had seen him like this before years ago when I was pregnant with my daughter, back when we lived in Fullerton. At that time, I didn't know what it was, and I didn't ask any questions. But this time was different. I confronted him and developed trust issues leaving my children with him in that condition. Eventually, I had to quit my job because I didn't trust anyone, including their dad, to watch my children if I thought they were in danger, which he wasn't intentionally bringing upon them.

Then came the eviction notice, as my job was our only source of income. I responded to the court order and received a court date for the eviction, but I missed it, resulting in a judgment against me. I had to move out of the home we had lived in for 5 years. With nowhere else to go me and my now two children ended up back at 5728, which I dreaded.

By that time, my grandma had passed away, and my mom had taken over the house. It was tough! When the time came, I had to pack up all my things, feeling like I failed my children as their protector. Depression hit hard. I found myself heading back to 5728 with two children, the very place I didn't want to go—the place I had avoided as much as possible, where hate seemed to seep from the walls. It was the place I knew I wasn't wanted, and now my mom had taken over. Lord, help me!

I had put most of my things in storage, including all my kids' keepsakes, which I ended up losing, deepening my depression. All I had were the things and clothes I took with me to 5728, while (CT) went back to 5512, just around the corner. Not only was my family separated, but I also found myself somewhere I swore I wouldn't return to. Depression hit me hard, and (CT) worsened with drugs.

I found myself back in my old bedroom, sharing a queen-size bed with my two children, doing everything I could to escape my mom, (CT), and my depression. My children were the only reason I didn't completely give up on life. I fell back into my old habits, hanging out with other men, smoking weed, drinking, and still doing my best to take care of my children.

I didn't allow (CT) to see my children at all because he was getting worse every day. Then one day, I snapped out of the slump the devil wanted me to be in. I told (CT) I didn't want to be with him anymore. The relationship had been over, I just hadn't told him because by then, **he had turned into a real live monster**.

(CT) kicked my mom's door in twice, completely off the hinges because I wouldn't let him see my children in the state of mind he was in at the time. But to him, I was keeping his kids away from him. He then tried to get my children taken away from me by calling Child Protective Services, telling them all kinds of lies. *It showed how little he truly cared for his kids.*

I wanted out of that toxic situation. Depression had set in so deep that I didn't realize a year had passed since I had been back at 5728. He would come to my mom's house in the morning because he knew she would be at work. One time, I caught him trying to jump the back gate, with one shoe on, looking like a real mess. He was totally unrecognizable; demons seemed to possess him. I was embarrassed to say he was my children's dad. The monsters in him didn't care; they just wanted to hurt me, even if it meant our children would end up in the system.

The lady from Children's Services showed up about 3 days after he called them. The first time she came to 5728, my children and I were at my uncle's house a few blocks away. When I returned home, my mom told me that a lady from Children's Services had been there and left a number. I couldn't wait until the next day to call her, so I called her first thing in the morning. I made an appointment for her to come back out. When she returned, she saw where my children and I were sleeping and checked the closet where all my kids' brand new clothes hung up (remember, I lost our things in storage, so everything was brand new). I made sure my **kids were well dressed**, and she also checked the refrigerator, where she saw that there was food in the house. She was surprised because he had called them and lied!

She asked my daughter if I rolled marijuana in front of her (she was 6 at the time), and my daughter said "no." So, the lady, my children, and I sat down on the couch, with my son sitting on my lap. The lady explained that she couldn't tell who had called and made the report on me. I told her I knew who had called because he had told me he was going to. I thought he was just playing around, but he actually called. Out of nowhere, my son, who was 2 at the time, said, "my daddy kicked in the door." Of course, **they are going to believe everything a child says, so immediately the tables turned! God had His own plans for this situation**.

The lady said, "What?" and my son repeated, "**my daddy kicked in the door.**" She said, "**I need you to get a restraining order in place in order for me to close your case, because it seems that their dad is a threat to them, and I need this done A.S.A.P! Or I'm going to look at this like you are not protecting your children.**"

That's all she needed to say; she gave me a week to get the restraining order. The next day or so, I was at the courthouse getting a restraining order. I believe the court informed (CT) of what was happening because when my court date came, he showed up, talking about how he loved his kids. So, we had to go to mediation before seeing a judge.

In mediation, we agreed to visitation with him and my children under supervision. **The judge granted the restraining order and our agreement,** and it was finalized. **<u>The lady closed my case, and I was free.</u>**

Since we lived around the corner from each other, (CT) would meet our kids at the corner near his grandmother's house with someone from my family (usually my mom or my sister). His whole intention was to see me, but by then, I hated him! My heart burned with hate for him, and I did not want to be near him. I got another job on the west side of town as a nutrition driver for Delta Sigma, and I got myself together. My mom and I had been having arguments. **<u>You've never really struggled until you're sleeping in someone's house who doesn't want you there.</u>** Plus, I was ready to pay my own bills again instead of giving her money on bills, and she was acting like I wasn't contributing to that house, like my kids and I were just laying up on her! **<u>God is so good</u>**; one day while doing my route, I found a 2-bedroom house for rent for $750 a month with the address 2223. I did what I needed to do to get that place.

Yes! I got the place with the help of the county. They covered my first and last month's rent, my U-Haul, my refrigerator, and paid my bills for 4 months. While I was going through the process of getting my place, sorting out paperwork between the landlord and the county for assistance, my mom knew nothing! Until about 3 days before I was actually moving. I said, "Mom, I'm moving," and she laughed, saying, "Girl, you ain't going nowhere," and that was the end of that conversation. Little did she know, I **already had the keys** to my house. I had been going there and cleaning it the way I wanted for me and my children. I had already ordered their bunk beds and my new refrigerator; I just had to pick them up with the U-Haul the county had already paid for. I had done everything but move in when I finally told her I was moving.

A few days later, she went to work, and when she came home that day, I was gone! My old room was completely empty. The only thing I left was my children's big, colorful map rug. The night before, she had gone to bed with no idea that my children and I would be leaving the next day, escaping from her toxicity and controlling ways, which was another reason I had to get out of her house. I was tired of her trying to dictate how I raised my children when she didn't even raise her own kids. **She couldn't tell me anything!**

I didn't pack anything; I moved everything as it was, including me and my kids' dressers with folded clothes still in them and clothes still on hangers. **God was taking care of me even when I didn't see it.**

By this time, (CT) had kind of cleaned himself up; he was starting to look like himself again. Looking back, I believe and know that the separation of our family affected him too. We just handled it differently. At the time, I couldn't see his pain because I was consumed by mine. We were both hurting, although he blamed me for his hurt, which he had no right to. He caused this entire situation to come into play with the decisions he chose to make, not thinking about his family when we were in our own place.

People often think that the things they do don't affect the people around them, **but they do!** Anyway, **nobody knew about these moves I was making in silence** (which has become a habit to this day), not even him. I told him the night before that I had a place for us, and he helped me move everything the next morning. I can't tell you the joy I felt that whole week and had to keep all that goodness to myself. I haven't been back to 5728 since; it's been over 20+ years. **I thank God and Jesus every day for keeping me under my own roof.**

When my mom finally came to my new house and saw how big it was and the area I lived in, I felt the hate heavily. I just smiled because she just knew in her own mind and heart that I was going to stay under that roof with her toxicity, but I moved right under her nose. She had been wanting me and my children out of her house; she showed that daily—**energy doesn't lie!** *People and their wicked hearts.* She came to my house maybe 3 times out of the 7-8 years I lived there, which was fine with me. The house I live in now, she has only been here maybe twice, and March 2023 made 15 years I've been here. **Thank you, Jesus.**

The moral of this story is profound:

People may express their feelings about you in hurtful ways, often without saying a word. Trust the energy that surrounds you. **True love doesn't inflict pain**; those who love you won't hurt you.

When you feel like you're navigating rough waters, remember that **God is quietly working in the background.**

Every trial you face isn't meant to harm you but to reveal the strength within you, known to God even when it's hidden from you.

Your current struggles are not your final destination; **keep moving forward**.

Even when it seems like you're drowning in pain, God is actually rescuing you.

The Holy Spirit, who raised Jesus from the dead, resides within you. Just as God revived Jesus, He will breathe life into your mortal body through this same Spirit.

Worrying cannot add a single hour to your life. Since you can't control even this small thing, why fret about the rest?

Luke 12:25-26

A Prayer for Truthfulness

Father Lord,

Please forgive my lying tongue. It has caused much pain and trouble. I have testified falsely, deceived others, and falsified documents for personal gain. I am truly repentant and sorry, Lord, and I am ready to make amends. I am willing to give up all I gained in exchange for redemption. Sanctify me, Lord, and make me new. Replace my deceitful tongue with one of truth. In Jesus' name, I pray. Amen.

Chapter 07:
2223 ½

Raising 2 kids, a man, and working nightshift

Days before I moved in, as I mentioned in Chapter 6, I did my own deep cleaning. I had six bottles of Awesome, bleach, towels, a bucket, and everything else I needed. Despite paying a $400 cleaning fee, I ended up cleaning the place to my liking. I isolated myself—nobody knew where I was. I didn't answer my phone; it was just me, my new house, and Pandora. It took hours to clean and admire my new home simultaneously. My children didn't even know we were moving until we did.

As I pushed open the wooden door to my new two-bedroom back house with a yard for my children to play in, a spacious front porch for me to relax on, and lemon and fig trees on the side, along with a clothing line if needed, I felt a sense of joy. The market was right next door, and the schools my children would attend were conveniently located. The house was 15 minutes away from my job on the Dash bus and an 8-minute drive. Everything I needed was within reach, especially since I didn't have a car at the time.

Anyway, as I pushed the door open, I saw everything I had moved piled up on the living room floor. Despite the mess, I was happy. Happy to be away from 5728, happy that the house was mine, happy to have two bedrooms, a kitchen, a back door, and a porch. I was happy to have my privacy back. Standing in that big living room, looking at the pile of belongings that needed sorting, brought me joy.

So, I sorted and placed everything where I wanted it to go. It wasn't until about 11 pm that night that I finished. I was glad to be done because then I could see what my living room looked like without all our things in the middle of the floor. It seemed even bigger than I remembered before piling all our stuff on the floor. I was tired but went to bed happily on my big queen-size mattress that sat on the floor in my room, which had two entryways—one from the living room and another from the hallway by the bathroom.

My children went to bed happily as well in their new home, on their brand-new red bunk beds that their dad put together while I was sorting and placing our things. Their beds matched well with their colorful drawers. I couldn't wait until the next day to wake up in my new house.

The next day, I transferred all bills into my name, went grocery shopping, and visited the schools to register my children. Despite all the moving tasks, I still had to go to work. (CT) came along with us, somewhat unsure about our relationship, with one foot in the door and one foot out. I hadn't made it clear that we were back together. All I knew at that moment was that I had my family, and he still had some proving to do. Him living with us was okay, especially since the kids were still going to school on the east side of town. We had moved to the west, where (CT) wasn't too comfortable, but he knew he had a place to lay his head with his children in the next room. He took our kids to school every morning until all the paperwork was done for them to attend schools near our new house.

The situation continued until I grew tired of him bringing my children home after 8 PM on school days. By then, my mom's husband had found a van for me, which I purchased for $700. It meant I had to pick up my babies every day after work and before dark. Before the next month's rent was due, my landlord passed away. I had moved in February, and she passed away before March arrived. **God knew the plans He had for me.**

She lived in the front house. I met her daughter, whom I didn't know existed. So, I started paying my rent to her. She couldn't deviate from the lease her mother and I had signed, which stated, "rent was due every 5th of the month, and the late fee was $3." Her daughter was **another monster** I encountered. She was rude and unfriendly (looking back, I now understand why). I had a light about me that I didn't yet recognize, while she had a darkness that she owned. Energy doesn't lie. **Dark and light** is like oil and water, it don't mix.

The daughter didn't like that my rent was $750, with only a $3 late fee. Over the 7-8 years I lived there, she raised the rent every year, but only by the state tax percentage, which amounted to $15-25 each year. She didn't have to raise the rent, but she did. By the time I left, my rent had reached $900.

The daughter had a boyfriend who looked much younger than her. They would arrive in an old black jeep-like car, and eventually, she started sending him to collect the rent. Although she was a good landlord when it came to fixing things promptly, dealing with her was challenging as a tenant. I preferred interacting with her boyfriend; it seemed like even then, God was intervening, knowing her true intentions. Despite paying rent every month, it was often paid late. The extra $3 didn't bother me much. God provided for me without me realizing it.

It reached a point where I juggled three part-time jobs simultaneously. I worked my primary job as a nutrition driver for four hours, squeezed in my second job during that time, then after my primary job, I worked my third job for another four hours. I'd complete my primary job's route two hours early, then work my second job for two hours before moving on to the third.

I felt restricted in my own home, where I paid rent diligently each month. I had a washer and dryer despite not being allowed, and my kids played in the front yard despite the rules against it. I even had pets, despite the no-pets policy. It seemed like she wanted me out so she could sell the place, which might explain why she raised the rent every year. But as long as I kept paying, she couldn't force me out. However, she kept raising the rent until it became unaffordable for me—or so she thought.

God blessed me once again when an opportunity arose to work for Metro as a service attendant. I did everything necessary to secure the job, and once again, I felt divine intervention at play.

By this time, (CT) was no longer living with me, and my children were attending school nearby. They were 11 and 7 years old. My assigned division at Metro was Division 8, known as the cleanest division in the entire Metro system, located in Northridge. My work hours were from 5:30 pm to 2:00 am.

This opportunity meant serious decisions had to be made for me and my children. It offered more money, better benefits, and a chance for a better life, as I was starting to struggle with my previous jobs, rent, and responsibilities. With this new job, I needed (CT)'s help, so I paid him to take care of his own children while I worked from Friday to Tuesday, including my off days on Wednesday and Thursday, until I completed my probation period of 120 days.

With the increased income, I could afford to pay him $150 every two weeks for looking after his children, which wasn't an issue for me. My priority was work, but I didn't realize that my children rarely saw me during this time.

Looking back, I realize I was prioritizing my job and money over my children's mental well-being and their feelings. Moving, making new friends, and my constant work schedule were taking a toll on them. We'd get home at 4 AM, only to be up again at 7 AM. It's no wonder my daughter struggled in school; now I understand where things began to change, and it was all my fault. I knew **I was providing a better life for us**, that's all I could see at the time, improved living conditions, even if it meant stopping at Jack in the Box on the way home in the 3 am hour.

Despite their suffering from not seeing me as much as they should have, they saw me hustling. To this day, my children get whatever they want. I was being the mother I needed, determined not to rely on anyone else. I thought I was making it happen on my own, but in reality, it was God's hand guiding me all along.

I reached a point where I grew tired of paying (CT) to watch his own children, considering he helped bring them into this world. So, I stopped, and he didn't want to watch them anymore. Once again, I faced tough decisions to maintain my job, my home, pay bills, and provide for my children independently. By then, both of my children were attending the same school, and when they got out at 3 PM, I had to be on the freeway headed to work.

I would wake up early enough to take my bath, lay out my uniform, clean the house if needed, and cook dinner. Then, I'd get ready for work, make their plates and put them in the microwave. I had both a landline and a cell phone; my daughter would call me to let me know they were home from school. I'd remind them to do their homework, eat, take a bath, lock all doors and windows, and be in bed by 9 PM. Yes, my children were home alone while I was at work.

I developed a relationship with my neighbor, so she would look after them or let them stay at her house until I got home from work. This routine continued for months because all I wanted was to provide for my children and maintain the lifestyle I had built with my good income.

Eventually, my daughter told my mom that she didn't want to be alone in the house anymore. So, my mom stepped up and started watching my children (for which I am grateful). I had to enroll them back into the school they attended on the east side of town, near my mom's house before we moved to the west.

By this time, my probation period was over, and I had passed with flying colors. My mom's offer to help came at the perfect time because my job was transitioning to a 10-40 work schedule.

Then, I worked 10 hours a day for 4 days a week (Saturday to Tuesday) and had 3 days off (Wednesday, Thursday, and Friday). For two years, my mom watched my children while I worked. However, I still had to provide for my children and pay her. Sometimes she'd ask me to cover a bill or two, which was fine—I had the funds, and I just wanted to work. No one had ever done anything for me out of kindness once I started taking care of myself. I've always paid my own way.

During my 4-month probation period, I worked every day without taking a day off. When I transitioned to a 10-40 workweek, I started work at 5:00 PM instead of 5:30 PM and finished at 3:30 AM instead of 2:00 AM. I'd get home at 5 AM. On my first days off, I slept for all three days. I didn't realize how exhausted my body was because I was motivated to earn money. Metro was offering overtime, so I worked on my off days during my probation period. I was earning my **regular pay** (which was twice the minimum wage), **differential pay** for working after 10 PM and 12 AM, and **overtime pay**. When I say I was winning! **I was winning!** and **I've been winning ever since!** God takes good care of me, and I trust Him to continue doing so.

However, while I was happy, my children weren't. Someone else was taking care of them, and it wasn't me. I was solely the provider at that time, but they would have preferred to have me around. I didn't understand that then because I was focused on earning money for them and myself. After a year of commuting to Northridge, I requested a transfer to be closer to home. A few months later, I got the transfer to Division 2, which is right off the 10 freeway, near San Pedro, just a block away from the metro station.

Before the transfer happened

- I trusted someone I once knew.

Let's rewind a bit. After spending some time at Metro, I got involved with (MD), who was already working there and had a family of his own. Despite his commitments, I didn't care; I got whatever I wanted. (MD) and I messed around and hung out for months. Then, out of the blue, (KH), with whom I had a past relationship during my "doing me" period, reentered my life unexpectedly and rapidly. This was the reason (CT) no longer lived in my home. (KH) made me choose between him and (CT). Since I hadn't seen him in over 10 years, was tired of (CT), and already knew what (KH) was like in bed, I chose him—unaware that I was making the biggest mistake of my life. **What's familiar is not always safe!**

I was still involved with (MD), who resided in Santa Clarita, close to my job. We were good together, and he even put his family out of the house to be with me. I was present when his girlfriend, accompanied by the police, came to retrieve her belongings. As per her request, (MD) and I stood outside while she packed. On my way out, I forgot to grab my purse from the kitchen counter. When we were allowed back in, my purse was filled with liquor, specifically Remy. My money and papers were wet. Looking back, I realized **God allowed those things to happen** because I wanted someone who belonged to someone else without considering the consequences mentioned in **Exodus 20:14 and 17.**

Despite these events, (MD) said, "You're stuck with me now." I knew I didn't want to be stuck with him, but a part of me felt guilty. So, he officially became my man.

He would spend nights at my house, and I would spend nights at his, where he had recently moved a few months before our drama unfolded. I moved some of my belongings into his place and helped furnish it according to my taste, with him footing the bill since he was making more money than I was due to our different job titles. We traded vehicles – he drove my van because of its powerful sound system, while I drove his Durango. I even used his car to pick up my children a few times.

We were living it up, and he introduced me to many new experiences. I learned a lot from him; he had a "live for today" attitude and treated money like it was nothing. He took me shopping, and thanks to him, I got my first pair of Jordans and some other stylish Nike shoes that I wore until they fell apart. My children's dad never bought me anything! Writing about (MD) brings back fond memories and puts a smile on my face. Anyway, we eventually went our separate ways, but not before...

As I mentioned earlier (or did I mention it?), (KH) and I met years ago at a continuation school I was attending. He was two years younger than me. Back then, I was drawn to gangsters and bad boys. We instantly connected. Surprisingly, my grandma and my mom liked him too. He had a great rapport with these two women. He could enter my grandma's room, sit on her bed, and have conversations with her. She always welcomed him to dinner and allowed him to stay over late. He was the first to effortlessly become a part of my family; he was quite the charmer. My mom even helped him enroll in another school when he got expelled from ours. Their acceptance of him made me love him even more. He visited every day, always had his own money, bought me whatever I wanted, and kept my pockets filled with cash. I never asked where the money came from, and he never disclosed it; he simply provided for me. I met his family, spent nights at his house, and things were good for a while. However, I began to see a different side of him – controlling, jealous, and manipulative, which became more evident over time. Then, he suddenly disappeared. Later, I learned he was in jail for selling drugs. Looking back, I realize that **God was saving me** **by removing him from my life,** but did I listen? Keep reading! I moved on, and a year later, I started my family.

Years had flown by, and suddenly my cell phone rings displaying an unfamiliar number. It was (KH). After all those years, he showed up at my grandma's house looking for me and somehow got my number from my mom. We talked on the phone, and he ended up with my address. Lord what had I just done? What was I thinking? Is what I asked myself. I didn't care; it was him, and he wanted to see me. I wanted to show him how much I'd grown over the years. He pulled up in a glittery orange car, wearing that same smile. Little did I know...

I ran and jumped into his arms. He told me he still loved me and wanted to be with me. I admitted I still loved him too and wanted to be with him, despite still being involved with (MD) and living with my children's dad at the time. (KH) made me choose. I think he knew I would choose him anyway, and I did. All the warning signs he had shown me years ago went out the window. In my mind, (CT) was gone; I just had to tell him, not considering my kids' needs, only my own. (KH) didn't move in, but he stayed over many nights. Eventually, my children warmed up to him on my days off.

Time passed, and once again, he disappeared. This time, I knew why, and this time, I was pregnant with his twins, whom I chose not to keep (and I'm glad I didn't). He called me collect on the landline whenever he could, which was every day when he knew I was home.

Unaware of how long he would be gone, I told him I was pregnant with twins and had terminated the pregnancies, causing him to hang up on me. A week or two later, he called again. I answered, but this call felt different—the tone of his voice, the things he said. I didn't recognize the person I was talking to, which left me feeling uneasy. I wasn't really tripping because (MD) made me forget about (KH), who was in jail and angry at me for getting rid of the seeds he planted.

One day, I was at home when (KH) unexpectedly showed up. We were both happy to see each other, hugged, made love, and I thought everything was forgiven. But one day, during a heated argument, I told him I didn't want to be with him anymore, and he left. I got ready for work, assuming everything was fine until I received a text hours later saying, "I just broke into your house to get my things." I replied, "Make sure you close my door when you leave!!!" and went back to work.

I finished work at 3 am and debated whether to pick up my children from my mom's or go straight home. I chose to go straight home. I pulled up playing my music loudly, unaware of what was about to happen. I got out of my van, gathered my things, and headed to my front door. As I approached, I noticed it had been broken into, but I didn't think much of it at the time.

I opened my front door, turned on the lights, and locked the door behind me. Putting my things down in the living room, I headed to my children's room just to check, knowing they weren't there, and to make sure no one was in my house. After turning on the lights and seeing nothing in their room, I closed their door. But before I reached my room, I remembered I'd left their light on. So, I turned around, opened their door, and switched off the light. Closing their door again, I headed to my room.

Entering my room, I took off my shoes and called (MD) to let him know I'd made it home, but he didn't answer. Hanging up the phone, I heard my children's bedroom door open. Listening to make sure I wasn't imagining things, with my phone still in my hand, (KH) walked into my room with an evil look in his eyes. I jumped off my bed and asked him, "What are you doing in my house?" He pushed me back onto my bed. I tried to get up, but he pinned my arms down with his hands. My phone rang (OMG!), and I knew it was (MD) returning my call. (KH) answered my phone. All I heard from my side of the phone was, "I'm on top of her right now." At that point, I fought to get him off me, but he had me pinned down with his knees.

Time passed, and he got up, insisting I get dressed. Finally, I had a chance to look in the mirror, and I was shocked by my appearance, by the way he treated me, by what he had done to me without any concern. When I looked in the mirror, I saw my eyes were purple, my lips were busted, his handprint was visible around my neck, and my hair was disheveled. I was unrecognizable. **That monster** took pride in making me look like that. He was proud that he had broken me, but I am strong! He took my van keys and forced me to ride around with him. Eventually, we ended up back at my house, and he still strutted around with his chest out. I hadn't noticed my bedroom window was broken from me kicking my feet while he was choking me, as I was trying to free his hands from around my neck, until **God sent help** in the form of my daughter. She called my cell phone; (KH) answered it and handed it to me. As he passed me the phone, he grabbed my car keys. At that moment, I didn't care; I just wanted to be rid of him. I explained what happened to my daughter and instructed her to tell my mom to call the police (which she did). I also called them, and they came out. Everything was left as it was; they took pictures and collected evidence. I had to go to the police station for questioning and for them to gather evidence from me because he had raped me, beaten me, and stolen my car (this was someone who claimed to love me). My account to the police led to (MD) becoming involved.

It bothered (MD) for many reasons. The police informed (MD) about what had actually happened. When I returned to work after healing, MD's first concern was if I was okay. (MD) had to go to court to testify to what (KH) said to him on the phone when he called. This created a divide between (MD) and me. He had never dealt with the police like that before. That was new to him. We went our separate ways. We saw each other at work and spoke daily, but the intimate part of our relationship was over (or so I thought).

Eventually, (KH) turned himself in, thinking he had violated his parole, and they kept him because I had a case against him for assault and rape. They later found my van on my mom's street a few houses down, with my car keys on the front seat. The police took it to collect more evidence. When he realized how serious things had become, he had his brother call me, asking me to lie and say he didn't rape me. I couldn't do it; he had to face the consequences of what he had done to me! Going to court was the worst thing, with no support, because I had to continue to live and speak of what he had done to me in detail. I went through that process alone. When all was said and done, he received 15 years for my case. Later, I found out that another young lady came forward and said, "He did the same thing to her."

That orange car he pulled up in when we first linked up was hers; she was going through what I did not know I was about to go through. **God had a plan for both of our abusers. It took me to bring it to the surface for her to come forward.** I assumed his brother did the same thing to her as he tried to do to me. Time got added on to the 15 years he got for my case. I haven't heard anything further about (KH), but I have forgiven him, yes! For me, not him. I will be contacted whenever he does get released, which at this point, I don't care. **God has His hands on me!**

As for (MD), we just stopped communicating, period. A while later, (MD)'s girlfriend called me to tell me she was back at home but in a nasty way. I told her, "I told him to tell her to come home," which **shut her up real quick**, and that was the end of all of them in my life. God takes care of people as He sees fit, and sometimes bad things have to happen to us for God to get the glory and for justice to be served to **a monster** who thought he could get away with harming people. I know for a fact that **nobody gets away with anything;** God takes care of the wicked in His divine timing, even when we want that timing to be when we want it to be. I look at that horrible day as a learning lesson about the decisions I made.

As I write this, (KH) is still currently in prison for the crimes he arrogantly committed. God will not allow any of my enemies to triumph over me; I don't care who they are and what they are to me. **I will always win in the end**, no matter what. **That is the God I serve!**

A week or two later, after everything had happened, I got my van back. It was parked on the street in front of my house. When I came out, I found a brick through my windshield and small rocks on the ground on the driver's side. Immediately, I knew who had thrown the brick – it was my children's dad. I can only imagine why, but I got it fixed that same day. I drove around the area where I grew up until I saw him, just to show him, what he did was nothing! I understood that his actions came from hurt and disappointment. Knowing he had heard about what happened to me, I let it go and kept living my life.

Two months later, God opened another door for me to move, and that was the end of 2223. I drove past it a few times after moving away, and each time, the grass was higher and higher. It started looking like the homeless were sleeping in the front and back house; it was surrounded by gates from the city. I guessed that after moving, the daughter sold it. I kept moving! Nothing can stop me! *I am no one's victim!* **When people show you who they are the first time, believe them** (factual advice). **Don't allow people to stay in your life longer than they deserve** (personal advice).

In the Bible, it says: **"The wicked will be brought down by their own wickedness." (Proverbs 11:5)**

The moral of this story is that I had who God wanted me to be with; I just didn't know it then. I couldn't see him because all those other men were blinding me. I didn't see his worth then, but looking back, <u>it was bright as day!</u> His pure love alone was worthy enough to trust God's process with us. <u>All he had to give me was love</u>, **true love**. As I write these words, tears run down my face because back then, my ego was too big to see his love even when that was all he had to offer. Honestly, I haven't experienced true love from any other man but **God's love**, and **<u>there is no greater love.</u>**

"You can't dance with the devil and wonder why your life is a mess." **(Matthew 3:8)**

Everything isn't greener on the other side; <u>it's green where you water it.</u>

Our selfish decisions will not only hurt us but also those around us.

Be careful what you ask for; God is always listening, and <u>he will give you what you want just to show you it isn't what you need</u>, **<u>in the way he sees fit</u>**.

Pray this prayer over your children daily in the name of Jesus, and he will do it!

"**Lord, I ask that you protect my children** spiritually, mentally, physically, emotionally, and **in every way.**

In Jesus' name, Amen."

<u>**My learning lesson**</u> from that part of my life was realizing that being a mother means knowing that, regardless

of whatever else I did or didn't do, I gave the world something beautiful.

Trusting the process

Nothing happens by accident, and even those things we wish we could take back bring us to the places we need to be. We are who we are because of the choices we made, not the choices we thought about.

God allowed that to happen to me just to show me who really loved me. I didn't appreciate it **because I was thinking with my vagina** instead of my head and my heart, **as the** devil **had programmed me to do**. The gift God had given me in the form of my children's dad, **I threw it away** like **the** devil wanted me to do **because he doesn't like unity.** Instead of holding on to it, although things were what they were between us, it was for me to help build a strong foundation that would have helped CT reach his greatness.

"Forgetting what is behind and striving toward what is ahead, I press on toward the goal to win the prize for which God has called me heavenward in Christ Jesus." **Philippians 3:13-14**

Love what you have before life teaches you to love what you lost.

I pray this story of mine touches someone who needs their eyes opened to someone that was/is sent by God and appreciate him or her, **in Jesus' name.**

Chapter 08:
It had to happen

I wanted more than I had, so I went after it, and then came the betrayal, slander, persecution, hate, and isolation from those who claimed they *loved me*—and this is after everything I had been through two months before God opened a new door for me. There I was, free of that monster I'd encountered. It had to happen.

This new door God had opened came as another two-bedroom, this time upstairs, downstairs. Months before I had moved from 2223, I had written a letter to Lahacla, submitted an application, and explained to whomever had got my application in their hands—one of God's angels—what I had gone through. In two months, I had my keys. I was still working at Metro, still driving to Northridge. I was still waiting for my transfer to come through, and it finally did. I had my keys for about three months before I moved in. Once a week, I would go to my new home to check my mail. I was still dealing with (md) sleeping at his place even after what happened at 2223. My children, meanwhile, were still with my mom. Me and the kids would go to our new house on my off days to eat and spend the night to get a feel of the area.

One night, while at our new house, I met someone I decided not to call until a month later. Our first conversation was magnetic; I called him one day on my way to work, and we talked the whole ride, which is an hour and a half drive, depending on the traffic. Long story short, that relationship lasted six years.

Here's my story.

***

On my last night at Division 8, driving home, my van started smoking right by Division 2, where I was supposed to start the next day. I drove to my mom's house, and my van was doomed when I got there at 4:30- 5:00 am. I had blown my head gaskets.

Starting at Division 2 wasn't looking good.

It's a good thing the metro was a 10-minute walk from my new home and a roughly 7-minute walk from division 2, making it super convenient. Thank God! I had to adapt to change immediately because now, I was on the train going to and from work. At the same time, *God still showed me his hand is on my life*. I now realize that none of what just happened was a coincidence; I never had any issues with my van driving back and forth to Northridge for almost two years, and then suddenly, on this particular night when I no longer had to drive out that far, my van broke down! I jumped on the train to work for about three months, my mom's husband would pick me up at 2 am and take me to the new house, that is until he got tired of waking up at 1:30 am to get me from work. No buses or trains were running when I got off.

One morning, he showed up with a little white car that was a *stick-shift*. He told me I could have it if I learned how to drive it, and within a week, I was up and rolling again. Now, I know how to drive *stick-shift* and *automatic*. By this point, my mom had reached her limit watching the kids, and since she needed a break from my responsibilities, I would pick them up from her house when I got off work at around 2:30 am. They still went to school by her house.

In those six years, I went through a lot with my daughter. However, at the same time, I also began to tap into my gifts and talents like cooking, which allowed me to start my catering business by the name of *Beautiful Eating,* which was the start of God showing me who among my family and friends was on my side and who was not.

To begin with, I started selling from my house, focusing on only chicken and fries; then, once I knew the profit was good, I started doing events, where the government paid me to feed people. I even started selling my loaded fruit jars—though they were originally called something else, before I was forced to change the name because I did not do my research first. These loaded fruit jars also made a nice profit. Everyone I knew wanted them and was requesting them. My homeboy from Metro ordered ten and took them to Las Vegas to his folks, which would have expanded my business, but then my family started hating on me. They could not contain their jealousy anymore.

Do you remember (Delilah) my uncle's girlfriend? Well, as it turned out she was stealing photos of my product off my Facebook page while I was advertizing and promoting myself. She was posting the stolen photos in private groups she was in on Facebook as if she was making the product herself, as if she was bold enough to do what I did on her own. No! She had to steal from me, then told me out of her own mouth. She and her sons had their own jealous plans but, by the time she told and showed me her get-down the company whose name I had accidentally used on my product emailed me and asked me to remove everything that mentioned their name on social media, or they would take me to court for copyright infringement. Which made me change the name of my product and get it patented along with the ingredients. I posted proof of my product that was then patented on my Facebook profile, letting any and everybody know that if they infringed on my product, I would sue them, family or not. Her sons began to act very disrespectful, trying to sell my product with their own ingredients. But they didn't have the skills to match mine, so that didn't last long!

My product also made my own sisters go against me, and side with a woman who had been jealous of me for years but, played victim.

Firstly, my sister Daisy came down from Bakersfield to visit. One day, we were at the park, where I was posted selling my product. I had asked her if she wanted to swing by and try one for free. At first, she refused, then she pretended like she didn't drink; and yet, only two days later she started promoting the product that was stolen from me on social media and tagged it as a family business. I was beyond pissed. I was not about to let that happen! This was *my business*—and family had nothing to do with it.

I let *that* be known all over social media.

Then, my other sister Scarlet opened her big mouth, talking about how it was *her* idea. Listen, every Sunday after church, we went to Scarlet's house for dinner and have wine and fruit. *Do you know how many people do that?* Her idea, my butt! With my brilliant mind, I took it to a different level and made it my product. She would *never* have made the move I made, and as far as I'm concerned, it was *never* her idea. It was just something we did every Sunday after church with dinner.

You see, they had put me in a *box*, one that I was simply outgrowing. Here I was, I was achieving things they didn't have the courage for. Everything I was doing, God was blessing—at the same time showing me who really wanted to see me win! And it was not my family. During all this back and forth on social media where they needed validation, they all teamed up against me. They didn't know God was using them for my greater good and purpose. I didn't even know. My sisters going against me was a joy for Delilah. She loved every bit of them publicly slandering me, persecuting me as she did the same. That hate and jealousy were coming from someone who used to braid my hair as a young girl—someone I thought could teach me how to be a woman. It was only later that I realized that you don't have to be half naked to feel beautiful, and she was half naked all the time. Girl, put some clothes on! Have some respect for yourself, *know your worth!* All she shopped for was skimpy clothes.

So, no; she wasn't the one to teach me anything.

Even my mom said, *"God was using me because I was the weakest link."* She sided with all of them, too. I will never forget those words she said to me, trying to hurt me, and as I look back, I laugh so deeply that my stomach hurts.

I tell you, as I write about this story, **I am stronger than all of them put together to this day!** I have accomplished things they will *never* do. They don't even believe in themselves enough to get the things done that I have! The devil used them to try and break me, and what's meant for evil, God will always use it for good.

Look at me now!

Not long ago, during the course of writing this book, I've had to block Delilah; she kept making different profiles, and those jealous demons she carries allow her to try to keep track of my accomplishments through my supposed family—though, of course, they can't tell her anything since they know nothing. I've learned that *moving in silence keeps the negativity away*. God will make sure they all get this book in their hands, in the name of Jesus.

At the thought of them seeing me continue to move forward despite their plans for my downfall, I'm humbled and at peace just as God would want me to be.

When you are focused on somebody else's blessings, you become ungrateful of your own.

As I write this, I feel sorry for all who have come up against me and are no longer a part of my life, which is now a privilege! I know they miss me because they realize **I was the light in their darkness**. <u>I loved them while they hated me</u>. God knows their true hearts and motives; but it was up to me to see them for myself, even if it hurt. They let my success get to them.

I will never fit in anybody's box. I'm different!

The moral of this story is ***people pretend well***. Trust the ***energy*** that is being shown to you instead. When problems, in the form of people try to break you, just bow your head and talk to God.

You will keep perfect peace all who trust in you.

All whose thoughts are fixed on you!

Isaiah 26:3

Chapter 09:
Having Family that's not Family

They hated me more than they loved me

Jealousy

It's sad but the naked truth:

Family ain't what it used to be.

Family now gangs up on other family members. There used to be a time when you could go to your grandma's house to get a plate, chill with your cousins, and get love form your aunts and uncles. Now, everybody chooses who they want to deal with. Aunts/uncles choose which kids to be proud of. Brothers and sisters treat friends more like family. Cousins talk about their own family members and don't realize they are the most flawed! Certain grandparents spend time with certain grandchildren. The only time you see family now is during a funeral! When there is a wedding, family reunion, or family outing, even then, they're fighting or talking about each other.

This is sad, but the truth needs to be said. No one is better than the next; we all come with imperfections! The cycle can only change when people decide to do better!

In the year 2020, the devil attacked me through my whole family, mom and dad's side. He used some to betray me; he used some to talk down on me; he used some to turn their back on me; he used some to have hate in their heart for me; and he used others still to reject me—from my mom, dad, sisters, relatives, aunties, grandma, and friends as well. It's sad because they were not mentally strong enough to fight against him and his plot to destroy me! It had to be done; nothing happens without God allowing it! He wanted me to see the people that surrounded me. People show you who they really are and how they really feel about you. **Family isn't always blood!** In many cases, even strangers supported me more than my own family.

I'm telling you this because this is how the devil operates. The devil uses people who already feel a certain way about you; that's what makes the betrayal, backstabbing, rejection, and isolation so easy. I don't trust *any* of my family with me; they have already shown me how they would treat me. They are all strangers to me now. Energy never lies. When we finally wake up, we see that we can only help each other out of situations if we come together to unite under one banner, under the name of Jesus Christ, working collectively together for the *greater good of our people*. This is the only way we will overcome the devil and the evil works that he tries to do to us daily. When you try to *destroy someone's life* with lies of any kind, take it as a loan: because it *will* come back to you with interest.

Family can sometimes be the most hurtful force in your life, and whoever said you have to tolerate that is wrong. It's the ones you love the most who can hurt you the most. You will have to choose between three paths.

I. You can <u>ignore</u> the pain and forgive;

II. You can <u>leave</u>; or

III. You can <u>remove</u> them from your life.

Any choice other than that is simply <u>self-inflicted pain</u>. God gave me the spiritual, mental, and emotional strength to do all four.

Know that each bad moment in your life is only temporary. You are so strong, and you have the ability to get through today, tomorrow, and every other day that throws you off.

Sometimes, family doesn't even love you for real. They just know you're a good person, and they would hate to see you loving another the way you loved them.

I've come to a point in my life where I silently remove myself from anyone who hurts me more than they love me, drains me more than they replenish me, brings me more stress than they do peace, and tries to stunt my growth rather than clap for it. I know that I've done more than enough talking and trying to make things work with certain people. I'm done!

Those who take action against you secretly but still stand beside you as though they support you, God will disgrace them openly.

- ➢ *Ask yourself,* has the way you have been living this life prepared you for the next life?
- ➢ Where would you like your soul to end up? There are only two places it can go!

Boundaries are your responsibility; you decide what is or isn't allowed in your life. *Boundaries don't prevent you from being the best version of yourself;* in fact, they allow you to be the ***best version of yourself.***

You are allowed to terminate your relationship with toxic family members, you are allowed to walk away from people who hurt you, and you don't owe anyone an explanation for taking care of yourself. There will always be people in your life who treat you wrong. Be sure to thank them for making you strong. People will throw stones at you! Collect them and build. They are helping you do the heavy work by throwing you stones that you don't have to carry.

Nothing others do is because of you. What others say and do is a projection of their own reality, their own dreams, and how they see themselves. Some of them can't even look in the mirror because of the reflection that looks back at them. Imagine looking in the mirror and seeing your character instead of your face. The daily torment.

The fact is, they didn't leave: *God removed them!* The reason why He removed them is because we prayed for goodness, and those people had none to give us. Some people are like clouds; when they disappear, it's a beautiful day.

Once the bond and trust are broken, there is no going back. The history doesn't matter. I know my worth! Sometimes, your humbleness makes people think they can play with you.

People always hurt the one that is sent to heal them, then wonder why they are always losing in life. The problem is people are being hated when they are real and are loved when they are fake. I've never shown fake love. The realness in me doesn't allow it. I never faked my care for anyone. I just stopped caring after realizing they weren't worth it.

People **love** the people who look *beautiful on the outside* and **hate** the people who *make their lives beautiful*. Your circle of family and friends is supposed to be proud, not jealous. Some people in your family will travel for miles away to bury you but won't support you when you are alive. Family is supposed to be your calm, your home, not another battle you have to fight. Sometimes jealousy isn't because of what you materially own; people envy how others love you, the vibes you give, and how you carry yourself.

It's dangerous to have jealous people around you. They look at you as competition while you look at them as family or friends. Know that they can't compete with you if you want them to win, too! They are actually fighting with themselves, for hate and jealousy are a heavy burden to carry.

Choose love. It's so much lighter.

Revelation 17:14

Don't allow people or anyone's <u>drama, hate, ignorance, or negativity stop you</u> from ***being who you are!*** Should you ever find yourself the victim of other people's bitterness, jealousy, lies, and insecurities. **Don't be mad**; things could be worse! You could *be* them! People *think* they can fix themselves by trying to break someone else. But a person who gets their strength from God *cannot be broken!*

Hate no one; no matter how much they've wronged you. Your greatest test will be how you handle people who mishandled you. **Stay kind.** The realest people get treated the worst but we *always win in the end.* And that's why I will always win in the end. You are not obligated to tolerate disrespect because the person is family. It's your family's duty to protect, not harm. When they fail to be a place of peace and comfort you are allowed to set boundaries to cultivate safety and protect your peace.

Manipulation hates boundaries.

Protect your peace!

Sometimes, the people you wanted as a part of your story are only meant to be characters in a chapter in your book. I have accepted the fact that people come and go *no matter who they are*.

Everything is temporary.

I lost everyone that was around me. Some, I chose to let go because God showed me they weren't good for me. I used to let people stay in my life longer than they deserved when I didn't know my worth. Now, my cut-off game is stronger than ever. I know my worth and my value. **I refuse to waste time trying to convince someone else of my greatness**.

People are quick to say, "I love you!" But they don't show it through their actions. When you love yourself, you'll stop settling for people who can't love you because you've set the standard to accept nothing less than the best! Don't say I love you if you can't say "I'm sorry!" Develop the eyes of an eagle, where you can see things coming from miles away.

I don't leave when it gets **hard**; I leave when it gets **disrespectful**. I refuse to have that boundary crossed again. It's a privilege to be a part of my life now; I'm super-expensive. If you can't afford my energy, I know you can't afford my presence. **People think it's disrespectful when you don't let them disrespect you.** Keep protecting your peace. Being calm when being disrespected is a *superpower!* I pray for whoever is reading this: I pray that anyone lying to you, using you, talking behind your back, and pretending to love you is removed from your life in Jesus's name!

You are not obligated to have a relationship with family members who are not good for your mental health. **Where there is <u>relational chaos</u>, there is usually a lack of boundaries.** The more chances you give someone, the less respect they'll start to have for you. They'll begin to ignore the standards you've set because they know another chance will be given.

Nope!

The fact is, they're not afraid to lose you because they know no matter what, you won't walk away, especially when you should. They get comfortable with it, depending on your forgiveness. **Never** let a person get comfortable in disrespecting you. There's a difference between a person who hurts you by making a mistake and a person who hurts you by continuing a pattern.

Mistakes can be forgiven.

Patterns should be *broken*.

If someone treats you badly, just remember: there is something wrong with *them*, not you. Normal people don't go around trying to destroy other human beings. In fact, *be thankful for the difficult people in your life.* They have shown you exactly who you should not want to be! If your heart hurts a little after letting go of someone or something, that's okay! It just means that <u>*your feelings were genuine*</u>.

No one likes endings, and no one likes pain, but sometimes we have to put things that were once good to an end after they turn toxic to our well-being. Not every new beginning is meant to last forever, and not every person who walks into your life is meant to stay! Negative situations may be a *reality*, but they're never a *finality*.

God can change any situation. Sometimes, you can *think* you're in a **crisis**, but you're really in the middle of a *miracle!* It's called a blessing in disguise.

So trust the process.

Never hate your haters; respect them, because they are the only ones who think you are better than them. What others say and do does not define you! People may have said bad things about you, but the good news is that people don't determine your future. God does. It is a perception of what they see and feel. You'll _never_ be criticized by someone who is doing *more than you*; and you will _always_ be criticized by someone who is *doing less*. Keep surpassing and outgrowing the box that people have tried to put you in. You can't force someone to respect you, but you can refuse to be disrespected. The truth is, life is **10%** of what *happens to you* and **90%** of *how you react* to it. I had to learn that myself! **Shout-out to the pain and the people who cause it: we had to endure in order to be great.** Those who I watched turn their back on me may they keep their back turned.

The streets didn't raise me to fold under pressure.

They taught me to *apply it*.

Jealousy is a nasty trait. It will have people hating on someone they should be taking notes and learning from instead of using their energy to try to tear them down. Having a jealous spirit will cause people to mistreat people that God sent to them to bless them. Everybody has a jealous **friend, family member**, or **associate**. The thing about those who have that jealous spirit in them is they act like they love you. Everything you do, they undermine it! Whatever you have, they want it too. They're always secretly in competition. And they pretend to wish you well. Be aware: everyone I had around me carried these traits! Their jealousy overruled their hearts. When they reveal themselves, give thanks. Now you know who they are. We hurt our own feelings, thinking we mean more to people than we really do.

Everybody *loves you* when you let things slide, but when you start checking things and creating boundaries, you become the *most hated*. I will not allow anyone to cross my boundaries! I stand strong on that! Some people really don't know how good you are to them until you remove them from your life.

Family isn't always about the people in your life who are blood-related; it's about the people in your life who want you in theirs. It's about the people in your life who accept you for who you are, support you in the things you choose to do, and, no matter what, are there for you. It's the people in your life who **love you**, **respect you**, and who you can **depend on**.

Now that's family!

Dear children, let's not say that we love each other.

Let us show the truth by our actions.

1 John 3:18

All of my family are now strangers to me. I love them from a distance, even if they don't love me back. Even those who have borne harm and wished harm my way I still love them, because I love myself. I love them because they're human like me. I love them because I won't judge them. I love them because I want them to love themselves, even if no one loves them back.

As a child of God, and as a warrior for Christ Jesus, I have to *love myself first* in order to love them. Love is when another person's happiness is equally important to your own. The fact is that everybody makes mistakes; the key is to learn from them with a positive intake. **A mistake that makes you humble is better than an achievement that makes you arrogant.** I'm not perfect, nor is the world, but I have learned to make things work for me, and I'm happy! Most of the happy people in today's time do not have drama in their lives. Maturity is when you are mocked, hated, and misunderstood, but you still serve, give, and love as if it never happened.

Karma says…

Don't be too happy **when people say they love you** and care for you. The question is: until when? Like the seasons, *people change.*

The moral of this story is: don't be afraid to lose people. Be afraid of *losing yourself* by trying to please everyone around you.

It's your own self-talk that determines how you feel. It's not about them; it's about *you! You* have the power to create the life you have always wanted. Choose to listen to yourself, not others. **Never** discredit your gut instinct. You are not paranoid; your body can pick up on bad vibes. If something deep inside you says something is not right about a person or situation, *trust it.*

Your life is a matter of **choice**.

And you have the **power** to take **action**.

I never have—and never will—let *anyone* stop me from being the best I can be, no matter what they say or do.

***

At my lowest all I had was God, and now I'm flying high like an eagle; I never worry about the next, because I'm too focused on my own nest.

Maybe that's why **I'm so blessed.**

Chapter 10:
Healing from Hurt

I separated myself from the toxicity that was surrounding me.

In September of 2020, another monster emerged in the form of my sister, Scarlet. She publicly persecuted, slandered, and betrayed me on social media, much like she had done once before in 2014. Life, as it often does, served as a profound teacher. When we fail to learn its lessons, they tend to repeat themselves. The persecution and slander I faced in 2020 were different, however, as I had become mentally, spiritually, and emotionally prepared. I saw it coming from miles away. Over the years, I developed the keen perception of an eagle, able to discern trouble on the horizon. I even shared my concerns with the mutual friends who were also acquainted with my sister prior to the incident. Yes, I had foreseen it all.

Before the storm hit, I had a heartfelt conversation with my younger sister, Jessica. I urged her to see beyond the influence of Scarlet and to love me for who I am, not for her convenience. But alas, Jessica was not yet equipped with the maturity to engage in such dialogue. She retreated to the comfort of Scarlet's shadow, eagerly awaiting the opportunity to unleash the venom that lay dormant within her. A person's actions often speak louder than words, and Scarlet's words overflowed with hate, jealousy, and envy. As the saying goes, "What the heart is full of, the mouth will speak."

To this day, I cannot recall the specifics of Scarlet's words. I merely skimmed through the posts and comments made by our mutual friends, recognizing that the sentiments expressed were far from loving. In those moments, all I could do was silently pray for her troubled soul. It's never the rumor that gets me, it's the audacity of the mouth it comes from. The family watched, fake friends watched, and the foes watched.

As the drama unfolded, both family and friends watched from the sidelines. Some out of genuine concern, others out of curiosity, and perhaps a few out of schadenfreude. It became evident that while many professed love, only a few were willing to demonstrate it through their actions. I found myself standing alone, abandoned by those whose loyalty I had once taken for granted.

Even relatives from Bakersfield attempted to assail me with their words, but their efforts were futile. I had fortified myself mentally and emotionally, recognizing that these trials were part of a divine plan. God was orchestrating my isolation, removing toxic influences from my life and forcing me to confront my own inner demons. It was a period of spiritual purification, a necessary precursor to the empowerment that awaited me on the other side.

Through solitude and introspection, I found strength. I confronted my fears, embraced my flaws, and emerged from the crucible of adversity with newfound resilience. Yes, I am now powerful, but not in the worldly sense. My power lies in my ability to navigate life's challenges with grace and authenticity, secure in the knowledge that I am guided by a higher purpose.

Everybody on my friends list was blocked and deleted. Some may have relished the spectacle Scarlet attempted to orchestrate. Social media fell silent, with everyone eagerly awaiting my response, reminiscent of the events of 2014. However, I refused to engage in the manner expected by Scarlet and others. I swiftly put an end to the entire charade without dignifying it with a response. Sometimes, the best response to rude, critical, and argumentative individuals is silence. Eagles do not stoop to the level of snakes; instead, they elevate them to their own domain, where the serpent's influence wanes, and clarity reigns. I understood that many anticipated my reaction, but I allowed them to speculate freely. I chose not to defend myself immediately because I trusted in God's timing and his unique way of vindicating me, as evidenced now through the medium of this book, where I can recount my truth.

Once, I felt compelled to rush to my defense against false accusations. Now, I observe quietly, discerning who stands by me and who succumbs to gossip. There are individuals perpetually consumed by anger and strife, but their battle is not with me—it is an internal struggle projected outward. While Scarlet believed her actions would wound me, they inadvertently became a blessing in disguise. Looking back three years later, I realize that the most challenging realization was discovering that those who mattered most to me valued me least. Yet, this revelation allowed me to purge my life of those who feigned affection, friendship, and support. I used to fear solitude, but I now understand that the true tragedy lies in surrounding oneself with people who breed loneliness.

Authentic kindness is selfless and consistent, devoid of hidden agendas. Those who honor their word and stand by their commitments are the ones worth keeping close. Scarlet's envy and jealousy, thinly veiled, were laid bare for all to see, revealing the true nature of her feelings toward me. Her actions merely echoed the sentiments harbored within her heart, as the biblical adage reminds us, "Out of the abundance of the heart, the mouth speaks" (Luke 6:45). I viewed her antics as a cry for help, a plea that remains unanswered to this day. Only divine intervention can provide solace for her inner turmoil.

Depression is a formidable foe, but through faith and prayer, I found deliverance. Today, I stand unburdened by despair, fortified by blessings, and shielded by heavenly protection in the name of Jesus. Rather than engage in idle gossip, I choose to devote my time to intercession, recognizing that God hears every prayer, even those whispered in secrecy. It is a truth often forgotten by many.

What went down also revealed something about my baby sister Jessica. Turns out, she feels the same way about me deep down. Even if I were to let her back into my life, she'd probably keep up the act. But she doesn't know that I'm onto her, starting this whole mess back in 2020 with her not bothering to listen and understand. I haven't brought it up with her though. I've just let it be, letting the man upstairs quietly shut that door.

I cut them off quietly, and they know exactly why. Truth is, I don't even miss them. When they had the chance to step up and be there for me, they did the opposite, even my own mom. I don't trust any of them with anything to do with me anymore. It's tough giving someone a second or third shot after they've already let you down once.

As I write this book, aiming to help folks like you overcome their demons just like I have, they're clueless about it. My appreciation comes from thanking them for giving me the inspiration to write this amazing book, thanks to their messed-up hearts and actions never lining up with their words. I'm wary of people whose actions don't match what they say. Actions always speak louder than words. I'm not accountable for how they feel because I was real about it. The devil tried to use them to bring me down, but the man upstairs turned it around to bless me big time. He's the boss when it comes to life's storms.

I know they probably miss me, but to be honest, I'm happier without them and their drama. People might think they played me, but in reality, they played themselves out of having a good person in their lives. It's a privilege for them to be part of my life now, and they blew it. Not all blessings come in the form of cash; sometimes, having folks who genuinely care about you is the real blessing. Once upon a time, I fell for the wrong crowd. But when the man upstairs removes the wrong ones from your life, it makes room for the right ones.

I'm walking into the good things the man upstairs has in store for me—peace, love, happiness, and a whole new outlook on life that's precious to those who lose it for the big guy's sake. He gave me a fresh start, and I ain't straying from this path.

"If you don't heal what hurt you, you'll end up hurting others who didn't hurt you. It's okay if healing involves shedding a lot of tears. Forgive yourself for not knowing what you didn't know before you learned it. The moment everything changed for me was when I realized I deserved better than what I was getting. Decide what you want, jot it down, make a plan, and work on it every single day. Part of healing is accepting that you'll never fully get it. Sometimes, you just gotta call it quits, not because you're mad or upset, just because you're done.

I was done wondering why my family kept trying to bring me down. I started asking myself why I kept allowing it. And I found my answer by setting boundaries and sticking to them. Another smart move made in silence. People don't realize how much you've had their back until you step away."

I've always kept my distance from those who don't deserve my time. There's no point in explaining my absence to someone who failed to value my presence. I've learned to reserve my presence for those who truly appreciate it. Not everyone will acknowledge your worth or the efforts you put in for them. I don't owe any explanations to those who have caused me pain. I stopped justifying myself when I realized that others only perceive things from their own limited perspective. Don't waste your words on people who deserve your silence. Silence speaks volumes.

I don't react with anger. Instead, I withdraw. I tried to love the people God placed in my life, but their negativity became unbearable over time. It reached a point where their toxicity outweighed any positivity. I don't mistake their avoidance of me for a personal issue; their vibes gave them away, and my intuition picked up on it. A person's energy can reveal more about them than their words ever could.

It's essential to keep your distance from those who refuse to admit fault and always make you feel like everything is your fault. Beautiful things unfold when you distance yourself from negativity and toxicity. Ignoring certain individuals is a crucial step towards inner peace. Life becomes simpler when you remove those who complicate it.

Maturity means knowing when to walk away from people and situations that threaten your peace of mind, self-respect, values, morals, and self-worth. Don't let past issues hinder your progress. It's okay to upset some people by making choices that are best for you. It's okay to do things alone and enjoy your own company. Being comfortable in solitude is a strength that few possess. Don't let your loyalty become a form of enslavement. If others fail to appreciate your contributions, let them fend for themselves.

When there's nothing left to say, it's okay to walk away silently. Silence can be powerful, especially when others expect you to react loudly. Learn to remove yourself from people's lives gracefully. If they fail to see your worth, it's their loss, not yours. Walk away from those who belittle you, from conflicts that lead nowhere, and from people who fail to recognize your value.

The more you distance yourself from toxic influences, the healthier your soul will be. Embrace solitude over fake company. Have the wisdom to walk away from nonsense. You can't shape your future if you're still tied to your past. Remember, sometimes it's better to let others lose you; they've had enough chances.

Respect yourself enough to seek peace and distance yourself from anything or anyone hindering your well-being. Taking a break from someone can help you realize what you truly miss or the peace you gain without them. Sometimes, it's best to step away until you can return with clarity and inner peace.

It takes great strength to choose solitude over poor company. Honor yourself by prioritizing your well-being. Waiting for someone to treat you right is a form of self-inflicted trauma. Removing yourself from situations where respect is lacking is an act of self-care. You deserve better; choose distance over disrespect.

Forgive yourself for lingering in situations you should have left long ago. Ask for healing from past hurts and seek renewal from a higher power.

There's a kind of beauty in the way strangers can become family, and family can fade into strangers; that's all part of the man upstairs' plan. Life takes on a new light when you release those who harbor jealousy, disrespect, and negativity toward you. I'm grateful to the man above for removing those who needed to be, both in the past and now, and for bringing the right folks into my circle. When you start seeing things through divine eyes, everything becomes clear. And you'll find that letting go isn't as tough as you imagined; in fact, it's a step towards your own betterment.

Don't waste your energy chasing after people; chase after your passions, your growth, and your dreams instead. Strive always to improve yourself, rather than trying to fit into someone else's world. Not everyone will celebrate your transformation, because it reminds them of their own stagnation. Life might seem eerily quiet just before all the doors swing open wide. I've come to understand that what feels like loneliness is often divine grace in disguise. So, take a breather, gather your strength; change is on the horizon.

Sometimes, cutting ties completely is the only way to safeguard your peace, and there's no need to feel guilty about it. Learning to be alone without feeling lonely takes time (trust me, I've been there), but once you master it, that's when true freedom kicks in. Some folks don't love you or care about you; they're just keeping you around for the perks, making the occasional call to maintain the connection until they need something.

People often underestimate the devastation caused when they push someone to give up on them, especially when that person genuinely loved them. It's a pain that's almost unbearable, driving one to tears, reflection, prayer, and ultimately, a decision to let go. Once I've let you go, you're gone for good—whether you're family, a friend, or an ex. The people in your life should be a source of relief, not added stress.

A narcissist will go to great lengths to impress a stranger, while treating their loved ones like dirt. Scarlet and others like her were just that—depressed, narcissistic monsters. After years of silence, I've come to realize that we're better off as strangers than anything else. I'm living my best life now, with the man upstairs right in the middle of all my adventures.

"Blessed are those who are persecuted for righteousness' sake, for theirs is the kingdom of heaven." (Matthew 5:10)

A prayer for gossiping…

"Father God in heaven, I've spread gossip and caused confusion. I spoke when I should've stayed silent, and I've betrayed the trust of loved ones. I've revealed secrets that weren't mine to share, breaking families and friendships. Please forgive me, Lord. Help me mend the bonds I've broken and dissolve any grudges that linger between me and my loved ones. In Jesus' name, Amen."

A prayer for being betrayed…

Heavenly Father, grant me the strength to forgive this betrayal. I relied on someone to be my rock, only to be let down when I needed them most. I thought I could trust them, but they proved me wrong, causing me immense pain. I felt consumed by hatred, but I know that's not the way. Help me release this burden and forgive them, just as You forgave me on the cross. In Jesus' name, Amen.

The moral of the story?

Well, I've learned plenty of lessons from a handful of messed-up folks.

I've come to understand that you can't change someone who doesn't see anything wrong with their actions. The only thing you can control is how you respond to them. If they treat you with respect, return the favor. But if they disrespect you, it's best to create some distance. Don't let the behavior of others tarnish your good manners because, ultimately, you represent yourself, not them. Once you realize your worth, losing people who don't appreciate it won't even faze you.

Always remember, you're accountable for your actions, regardless of your emotions. Be cautious with the notion that people are easily replaceable. Some individuals only cross your path once in life.

Never inflict harm on those who only want to see you happy. You can't go around hurting people and expect your life to go smoothly. Nope, it doesn't work that way. Some tears carry significant weight. Selfish individuals forfeit much in life because even when they recognize their errors, they struggle to seek forgiveness or express remorse.

You must possess the maturity to acknowledge your mistakes, the wisdom to learn from them, and the strength to rectify them.

Those who keep it real prioritize respect over popularity. While you can't choose your family, you can choose who you allow into your life. You don't have to tolerate toxicity, regardless of its source. Always safeguard your mental well-being at any cost.

"Monsters are real; they reside within people, and sometimes, they prevail."

Chapter 11:
Being Chosen and Blessed by the Hand of God Himself

The start of my spiritual journey and soul mission

In August 2014, I underwent baptism, marking a transformative moment in my life. Everything changed – my mindset, my perspective on life, my sinful habits, my very existence. I was oblivious to the spiritual journey ahead, but God knew. He had chosen me long before my birth. Only He knew the right time for me to renounce my wicked ways, my sinful behavior, my pride, and embrace the person He had designed me to be.

At the moment of surrendering my life to Christ, I remained unaware of God's grand design for my life. I merely answered His call. Fast forward to 2023, and I stand as royalty in the spiritual realm. I am untouchable, empowered beyond measure, bestowed with numerous divine gifts.

Upon surrendering my life to Christ, I had to crucify my flesh, forsaking its lusts and desires, dying with Christ to sin. I am liberated from the shackles of sin, witnessing the fruits of my repentance as I emerge from the depths of my former self. I have conquered lust, pride, and the allure of this world, obedient to God's word through the indwelling of His Spirit within me. I am grateful for this transformation; nothing holds sway over me anymore.

Trusting in God brings about change. Initially resistant to relinquishing control, I was accustomed to steering my life independently. However, upon surrendering the reins to God, blessings poured forth abundantly. Opportunities arose effortlessly, doors previously shut swung open, and my income soared unexpectedly. I now boast multiple streams of income, a testament to God's provision. Initially overwhelmed by the rapid pace of blessings, fear momentarily gripped me, causing me to veer off course. Yet, in surrendering to God's divine plan, I find solace in His guidance.

I am content to occupy the passenger seat, relinquishing control to God. Knowing that He guides me to unprecedented heights fills me with peace. Entrusting God with His wondrous works affords me tranquility of mind.

Philippians 4:19 reassures us: "God shall supply all your needs according to his riches in glory by Christ Jesus."

The same God who looks after me will provide for you abundantly from his boundless wealth. God always finds a way for both you and me. However, God needs to know he can trust you with the blessings he wishes to bestow upon you. Patience is key, as emphasized in Isaiah 40:31. I fearlessly entrust my uncertain future into the hands of my all-knowing God!

• Reflect on what inhibits your trust in God and Jesus Christ. Be honest; God already knows.

• Consider this: Jesus offers life, while the streets lead to destruction or imprisonment. What advantages do you see in that lifestyle?

• To the men and women of the world, ask yourselves why you turn away from the giver of life to surrender your lives to the one who seeks to destroy. Answer honestly, so God can reveal his hand to you.

Remember the words of 1 Peter 3:12: "For the eyes of the Lord are over the righteous, and his ears are open unto their prayers."

• **Trust God in all things,** even in times of suffering, knowing that it is temporary and serves a purpose. Trust in your healing process, and God will reveal his plan to you. In today's world, God has shown me the importance of reaching out to the forgotten souls, guiding them towards righteousness. True fulfillment in a relationship with God comes not only from personal purification but also from empowerment, enrichment, and divine guidance.

• **The notion of being chosen** by God is often romanticized, but the reality is far from glamorous. Being chosen entails enduring pain, bearing significant responsibilities, and facing spiritual battles against the forces of darkness. It involves confronting witches, warlocks, and their malevolent arts, enduring trials and tribulations, and experiencing envy, hatred, and persecution. However, being chosen also brings supernatural gifts, abundant blessings, divine protection, and profound peace. Despite the hardships, I fear nothing, for I am a blessed and anointed child of God.

• **Much is entrusted to those whom much is expected.** The fields are ripe for harvest, yet the laborers are scarce!

God Himself will reach out to you, revealing that you have been chosen for His divine purpose and glory. Understanding this entails recognizing that nothing revolves around your individuality; rather, all things serve God's purpose, and you are but a vessel in service of His kingdom. Whether acknowledged or not, God governs all aspects of existence, including every human being. Those who have perennially felt like misfits—the outliers, the black sheep, the indigo children, the outcasts, the star seeds, the loners— are indeed the chosen ones. No matter how hard they try, they simply cannot conform. Embrace this reality, accept it, and honor it. You were not born to blend in. When you genuinely follow Christ Jesus, the world will scorn you, mock you, slander you, test your faith, attempt to dismantle your sanity, and lay blame on you for all woes. Not everyone is cut out to be chosen. The chosen ones do not shed tears in front of others, nor do they display signs of weakness or vulnerability. To remain chosen, one must conquer "all" monsters, predators, and adversaries. The chosen are afforded no respite, no days off. Not everyone possesses the fortitude to be chosen.

• **Read Deuteronomy 28 for elucidation.** May this enlightenment provide you with comprehension and resonance. This is me expressing love through actions, as articulated in 1 John 3:18.

God revealed to me that without self-love, you'll be trapped chasing after individuals who will never reciprocate your affection. I needed this revelation! Cease talking yourself out of opportunities due to feelings of unpreparedness. The time is now! If you wait until you feel ready, you'll be waiting indefinitely. Immerse your mind in God's teachings, leaving no space for Satan's deceit.

At times, God may place a Goliath in your path to unveil the David within you. Some lessons can only be gleaned amidst storms. Occasionally, God sends tempests to underscore His role as the sole refuge! God leads you through turbulent waters because He knows your adversaries can navigate your level of tranquility. Sometimes, these troubled waters serve to purify us from the demons surrounding us, emanating from within us, and scheming against us.

I have slain the version of myself that mirrored the devil and have emerged as the woman God destined me to be. God stood by patiently, lavishing love upon me, awaiting my self-love. The one within you is mightier than the one in the world, as affirmed in 1 John 4:4-6.

Even if I were to lose everything today, I would still have God! That alone is sufficient to embark on a fresh start. I have embarked on numerous new beginnings. I shifted from venting to praying because I required strength to move forward, not sympathy. The key is to persevere! You lack nothing; utilize the gifts bestowed upon you by God! Falling in love with God ranks among the most rewarding experiences I have ever known! God's timing, God's method, God's narrative, God's glory! In Jesus' name, Amen.

• **Placing faith in God alters the course of everything!** I believe in God not due to parental or ecclesiastical influence, but because I encounter God's benevolence and mercy daily! God broke me down solely to rebuild me stronger than before. God may shatter your heart to redeem your soul. One must remember that the purpose of this life is to prepare the soul for the afterlife, as delineated in Isaiah 60:22.

Let's discuss genuine love! Nothing surpasses it!

Speak these words aloud and affirm them over yourself: "God, I surrender my reputation to you. I refuse to expend energy worrying about others' perceptions of me. I shall embrace my authentic self, allowing you to guide me in accordance with your will. Others' opinions are their prerogative! In Jesus' name, Amen."

You cannot anticipate God to rectify what you withhold from Him. Refer to Psalm 18:2 for solace, encouragement, and motivation. Focus on the doors God has opened for you, disregarding those slammed shut by others. When you maintain focus, people will react strangely. Let them. Sometimes, God isolates you to underscore that He is the sole companion you require! Regardless of who enters or exits your life, God remains an everlasting presence.

I implore you to draw nearer to God! Jesus is the path! There is no alternative route! A single prayer possesses the potential to alter everything. Prayer exerts formidable influence; however, bear in mind that God operates according to His timetable, not yours. Exercise patience! Revel in the Lord, and He shall grant the desires of your heart. Await the Lord's timing with patience. Be resolute and steadfast, yes! Wait expectantly for the Lord, as delineated in Psalm 27:14.

Recite this prayer as you await the Lord's timing:

Dear Lord, I stand in faith, confident that all circumstances will align according to your perfect timetable. Thank you for granting me the patience to await your divine intervention.

Never underestimate the power of a single prayer! While churches provide a traditional setting for prayer, the truth is you can pray anywhere—whether it's in your garage, car, amidst the mountains, under the shower's stream, on the dance floor, in your workplace, or even on buses. God and Jesus are omnipresent, listening to your prayers wherever you are.

Reflect on 1 John 2:15; it carries a profound message.

The Holy Spirit acts as your guide, offering warnings along your journey. It's crucial to heed these warnings. A Christian walking in the spirit may clash with those living in the flesh and immersed in worldly pursuits.

Consider the unparalleled life of Jesus, the greatest man in history. Though he possessed no earthly possessions or titles, he was hailed as master, teacher, and healer. Despite facing crucifixion, Jesus conquered death and lives eternally. He beckons you to emulate his example.

The decision to separate oneself from the world and carry the cross requires introspection. Are you willing to make this commitment? Respond honestly, and ponder why.

Be mindful—Jesus Christ's return is imminent. The thought of hearing "depart from me, I never knew you" should stir you to action. True love is exemplified in Jesus's sacrifice on the cross, offering redemption even to those who may reject Him.

As you engage in this reading, recite the following verses to fortify your faith:

- Isaiah 54:17

- Deuteronomy 28:13

- Psalm 18:2

- Psalm 20:7

- Romans 8:37

- Philippians 4:13

- Job 13:15

- Psalm 27:1

We may not comprehend God's plans, but we trust in His unwavering guidance. Prayer should not be reserved solely for times of need; express gratitude daily for His blessings. In moments of silence, trust that God is orchestrating something beautiful in your life.

Embrace God's promises:

1. Isaiah 41:10

2. Jeremiah 33:3

3. Philippians 4:19

4. John 14:27

5. Jeremiah 31:3

Know that God's love is everlasting, drawing you close with loving-kindness.

In solitude, find solace in God's comforting presence. He uplifts you when you feel depleted, becoming your everything in moments of despair. Take time to thank God for His protection and the gift of each new day. Seek stillness to hear His voice and rejuvenate your spirit.

Remember, mercy is when God withholds the punishment you deserve, while grace is when He blesses you abundantly despite your shortcomings. **Ephesians 2:4-9**

Psalm 90:12 reminds us of life's brevity and the importance of wisdom.

Recite the prayer: "Dear God, Grant me purposeful days, Restful nights, Peaceful home, And fruitful efforts. In Jesus' name, Amen."

You might not be blessed with all the resources or the full team like others. Finances might be tight, but let me shift your perspective. Look beyond the surface; things aren't always as they seem. Stop fixating on others and wasting time on things that don't matter. Walking with God is your ultimate strength, your lifeline in this chaotic world. I pray you realize the power in that, especially in today's times. God has orchestrated miracles in your life, even where you felt inadequate. That's His way with those who truly love Him; He shows up and works wonders. Walk alongside God, my brothers and sisters. I assure you, it'll be the most transformative decision you'll ever make. There's only one intermediary between us and God, and it's not a pope, pastor, priest, or prophet—it's Jesus Christ, our Lord. He goes before you, never leaving your side. Fear not, for God's got you covered.

Even in my darkest moments, I see God's blessings. His ways may not align with ours, but His plan for your life is flawless. Trust in Him!

The era of true worshipers is upon us, those who worship the Father in spirit and truth (John 4:23). I adore God because, despite my unworthiness, He showers me with His abundant blessings. He holds me in the palm of His hand. Being in love with God brings unparalleled joy, free from pain and disappointment.

Regarding the church and its leaders, my dear brothers and sisters, I can't address you as spiritually mature individuals but as worldly, still infants in Christ. I've fed you milk, not solid food, because you weren't ready for it—and you still aren't. Your worldly ways, marked by jealousy and strife, betray your spiritual infancy (1 Corinthians 3:1-3).

Living by the Spirit bears the fruits of love, peace, patience, kindness, goodness, faithfulness, gentleness, and self-control. Those who belong to Christ have crucified their sinful desires and live by the Spirit (Galatians 5:22-26).

Let's not become conceited or provoke envy but walk in step with the Spirit—doing good to all

Brothers and sisters, if someone stumbles into sin, restore them gently, bearing each other's burdens and fulfilling Christ's law. Don't deceive yourselves; God cannot be mocked. Reap what you sow, whether to please the flesh or the Spirit. Let's not grow weary of doing good, especially to fellow believers (Galatians 6:1-10).

In humility, value others above yourselves, echoing the mindset of Christ Jesus. Look not to your interests alone but to the interests of others (Philippians 2:3-5).

Strive for perfection, following the example set by our heavenly Father (Matthew 5:48). The Lord alone is our Savior (Isaiah 43:11).

Read this prayer aloud:

Thank you, Lord, for all you've done for me. Forgive me for my sins. Be the master of my life. Create a pure heart and renew my spirit within me. Heal the wounds of my past. I love and need you. Cover me, my children, my family, my friends, and my endeavors with your precious and holy blood. Grant me your dreams. Bless and protect all who seek, need, and believe in you. In Jesus Christ's precious and Holy name, Amen.

Prayer serves as a conduit connecting our overwhelming anxiety to God's overcoming power.

Midnight Prayer for Spiritual Strength:

Heavenly Father, Grant me strength to discern the spiritual battles surrounding me, to break through barriers and gates obstructing my path. Open my eyes to true friendship. Strengthen me to resist evil and live to honor you. Fill my heart with your wisdom. Let me rely on you in all things. Guide my decisions according to your will. In Jesus' name, Amen.

Midnight Prayer for Purpose:

Dear Lord, Clarify my purpose and reveal my strengths and weaknesses. Show me the meaning of my life. Guide me to live in accordance with your will. Help me surmount challenges and touch others' lives positively. Enable me to realize my potential and never lose faith in my abilities. In Jesus' name, Amen.

Midnight Prayer for Family:

Dear Lord, I lift up my family to you tonight. May your presence precede them wherever they go. Bless them in their endeavors, health, and studies. Shield them with the blood of Jesus. Fight battles on their behalf and safeguard them from unseen dangers. Grant them strength and fulfill their desires. Prosper them and illuminate their paths. In Jesus' mighty name, Amen!

Chapter 12:
The Revelation

God whispered to me, urging me to cease the futile struggle for a relationship that was never meant to be. The Battle of Forgiveness ensued, a skirmish fought within the depths of my soul.

For years, I waged war to forge a connection with my mother—a bond she remained unwilling to reciprocate. God unveiled the truth: my mother harbored jealousy towards me, a resentment she vehemently denied, even to this day. Her actions, both past and present, coupled with the words she uttered, painted a vivid picture of her envy. God, in his omniscience, bore witness to it all.

Three years ago, amidst the chaos of my inner turmoil, God intervened, commanding me to relinquish my quest for maternal affection. He revealed that the mother I longed for was but a mirage, obscured by the generational curse that tainted our family bloodline. My resilience merely served as a mirror reflecting her own inadequacies.

I've achieved numerous milestones in my life, yet the coveted words of maternal pride remain elusive. I've come to terms with the reality that her acknowledgment will never materialize, even as I pen this remarkable book, unbeknownst to her. I resolved long ago to pursue my aspirations for my own sake, indifferent to her approval. The woman she once knew has metamorphosed into a stranger, a fact she seems content to disregard—a sentiment I reciprocate.

When she calls, I seek divine guidance, allowing God to speak through me, yet her ears remain deaf to his message, tainted by the familiarity of my voice. Meanwhile, I continue my journey, concurrently crafting this manuscript and honing my skills as a professional nail technician while remaining steadfast in my employment at the construction company.

She remains oblivious to the intricacies of my life, indifferent to my accomplishments. And I've made peace with it, recognizing that her happiness for me would be a fleeting facade. Countless attempts to share my joys with her only resulted in dismissal, leaving me to rue my openness.

In a moment of clarity, God unveiled the root of her emotional aloofness—a legacy of neglect perpetuated by my grandmother, her own mother. The absence of love in her upbringing elucidated her inability to reciprocate affection. As I reflect on my childhood, devoid of maternal warmth, the pieces of the puzzle fall into place, illuminating the path to healing.

The journey of introspection, forgiveness, and self-love has been arduous, yet indispensable. Only God bears witness to the depths of my transformation.

A Prayer for Your Redemption:

Dear Lord, in my negligence, I have forsaken those in need, consumed by selfish pursuits. I've shirked my responsibilities, forfeiting years of love and connection. My children have grown without my guidance, and I've failed as both a parent and a member of my family. I've squandered the gifts you bestowed upon me.

I humbly ask for your forgiveness, that you may touch the hearts of those I've wronged, softening them to grant me forgiveness in turn. Guide me on the path to redemption, that I may reclaim what has been lost. In Jesus' name, Amen.

In July 2020, I graduated as a Medical Office Specialist. God orchestrated a moment when my mom bought me a graduation card that read, "One woman can change the world," and all my siblings signed it. It was a gesture that caught me off guard because, deep down, I knew my mom never truly believed in me or had faith in my abilities to purchase such a card from her heart. To this day, I'm not sure why she did it. She probably doesn't even remember buying the card, but I still have it—the sole card adorning my dresser. Everything, I believe, happens according to God's purpose and for His glory.

Yet, despite this seemingly celebratory moment, my mom's acknowledgment felt artificial and insincere. Simultaneously, my sister Scarlet's jealousy became apparent upon seeing the card, especially when she noticed the $200 inside. Her envy couldn't be contained, and she blurted out, "Do I need to go to school and graduate?" The subtleties may have escaped others, but I'm attuned to energy, and hers was unmistakable. Nevertheless, nothing was going to overshadow my day of triumph. Even after Scarlet's envious outburst, both she and Jessica attempted to latch onto my celebration. However, I distanced myself from them—I didn't want their negative energy around me. Instead, I celebrated with my children for the rest of the day.

Moving forward, I am determined that my daughter will never experience what my mom made me feel for so many years. She will never be belittled or discouraged. I will consistently uplift, inspire, and instill confidence in my daughter, encouraging her to be the best version of herself. I will rejoice in the opportunities that God presents to both of my children. They will have whatever they desire. I love both my daughter and my son equally, without favoritism. I am committed to being the kind of mother my children need, knowing that God chose me for this purpose. The toxic, demonic generational curses end with me, in the name of Jesus.

Be the beacon of warmth and acceptance for others, offering them a sense of belonging, visibility, validation, love, and support. Break the cycle of negativity and hurt.

If you were judged, choose understanding.

If you were rejected, choose acceptance.

If you were shamed, choose compassion.

Be the person you needed when you were hurting, not the one who inflicted pain. Pledge to rise above what broke you or attempted to break you. Embrace healing instead of harboring bitterness, allowing your actions to be guided by love rather than pain.

It wasn't easy, but I had to forgive—for myself (the battle of forgiveness). Understanding the essence of forgiveness took time. I often pondered how I could forgive someone who deliberately hurt me. However, through introspection and divine wisdom, I realized that forgiveness isn't about condoning or justifying someone's actions. It's about releasing the hold their toxicity has on my heart. It's been a journey, but I now comprehend and value it. So, I pray, "Lord, don't move the mountain, just give me the strength to climb it."

Those who dare to walk alone often find themselves in uncharted territories. Discipline entails doing what's necessary, even when it's challenging. Admitting wrongdoing and expressing remorse are signs of maturity. Pride may inflate, but no one has ever suffered from swallowing it. Remember, you can't expect God to mend what you're unwilling to surrender. Sometimes, forgiving in silence and severing ties is an act of self-care.

I'm glad I did it—no one holds power over me. Surrender your burdens to God's hands—remove anger, regret, worry, resentment, guilt, and blame. Clinging to these burdens only weighs you down. Trust your intuition, a gift from God, and travel light. You'll witness improvements in your health and life. We grow wiser not solely through years but through life's trials. Let go of preconceived notions and embrace the present. Your happiness begins now, in this moment. Dwelling on the past inhibits a brighter future. Your breakthrough may arrive when the odds seem stacked against you. Don't let life's challenges deter you; every success story begins with humble beginnings.

The side effects of focusing on yourself are profound:

1. Less drama

2. Numerous accomplishments

3. Abundance in every facet of your life

4. The life you deserve

Consider seeking guidance from a life coach if you find yourself in need—I did! Now, I could even become one myself if I chose to, haha!

Forgive yourself for the naivety that led you into the path of those who betrayed you. Sometimes, a kind heart fails to discern the deceitful. At this juncture, forgive the person you once were when you chose growth. Every encounter serves a purpose: either they alter your life, or you impact theirs. Forgive them, even if they seem undeserving; not for their sake, but for yours. By doing so, you release their grip on your life. Trust me, they lose no sleep, but you do. The wicked find rest only in causing chaos—it's written! I've ceased fretting over matters beyond my control and instead focus on my intelligent responses. Let go of the old to make room for the new, whatever that may entail for you. I don't know who needs to hear this, but move on, dear; they don't deserve your energy. Let it go! Attempting to comprehend why things unfolded as they did will only drive you mad. Your peace matters more. You can forgive someone without maintaining contact—it's not holding a grudge; it's preserving your peace of mind. I forgive and have forgiven people for my sake, allowing me to move forward without their presence. There's strength and power in both. My mantra? "I forgive you; we needn't stay in touch." I'm content with moving on! Sometimes, you must let people dwell in their negative world with their toxic energy and negative bank accounts because they refuse to grow. Be good-natured, but don't waste time proving it to others; they see your goodness, as does God. Don't feel disheartened if people remember you only when they need you. Feel honored; you're like a candle that illuminates their darkness. If your heart aches a bit after letting go of something, that's okay—it means your emotions were genuine. Endings and pain are unpleasant, but sometimes, we must terminate once-positive aspects when they become toxic to our well-being. Not every fresh start is perpetual, and not every person who enters your life is meant to stay—including family you didn't choose to be a part of, but God placed you here for a reason.

Don't allow these three things to govern you:

1. People

2. Money

3. Past experiences

Forgive those in your life, even if they offer no apologies; therein lies strength. Refrain from seeking vengeance; the rotten fruits will fall on their own. Find peace within yourself, even without the apology you seek—it wouldn't suffice, and it doesn't dictate your destiny. Reflect what you wish to receive. If you desire love, give love; if truth, be truthful; if respect, give respect. Your actions will always yield reciprocity. I could've reciprocated the treatment I received, but there's no reward in that—I'm wise. Hurting them back won't provide solace or resolution; it'll only exacerbate matters. Remember, revenge is never the solution. Regardless of how much they've wronged you, you're better than that. I once believed communication was paramount, but I've come to realize comprehension holds greater significance. If they fail to understand you, your message won't resonate, for they're not on your mental wavelength. Most people listen to respond, not to understand. A person's true character will invariably surface; I'll safeguard my peace instead of exposing their colors. I've smiled at those who uttered vile things about me, and they think I'm oblivious—joke's on them! Their words hold no sway over me. Love no one, regardless of their transgressions; live humbly, irrespective of your achievements; think positively, despite life's challenges. I'm imparting lessons on survival—I stand firm in my faith; nothing can shake it!

Reminders to keep close:

1. View failure as a new beginning, not an end.

2. Pursue what you desire, for it won't come to you otherwise.

3. Exceed expectations consistently.

4. Assume nothing; question everything.

5. Make peace with the past, or it'll haunt you.

6. Act instead of overthinking.

7. Refrain from comparing yourself to others.

8. Share your knowledge with others.

9. Forgiveness doesn't alter the past—it shapes the future!

Chapter 13:
Embracing Self-Love

The transformation within: a journey to self-acceptance

Overcoming pain to embrace peace and love

Always knew I could; just needed a guiding hand

I yearned for change, so I became the change I sought. One morning, I awoke with a resolve to banish the lingering pain from my life. Thus, I transformed, from the depths of my soul outwards, guided by the light of God/Jesus. It was a decision that reshaped my existence, the most pivotal move I've ever made. Those who embrace Him find true liberation. Rewrite your story; the prologue has already been penned. Never compromise your essence to fulfill someone else's needs. I relinquished the facade of mere allure; now, I nourish the souls of humanity. My path diverged, shedding those who couldn't appreciate my authenticity. Loyalty is immutable; we simply cease investing in those who fail to reciprocate it. It's better to stand alone than to lose oneself in conformity. I was not born to conform; I take pride in the woman I've become, forged through trials and tribulations. Never apologize for the depth of your love or the speed at which your heart embraces it. Love authentically, unapologetically, and without reservation. The tears ceased long ago, for it wasn't I who lost them, but they who lost me. Don't lament outgrowing those who chose stagnation over growth. Not everyone merits your benevolence. Learn to exude serenity and demand respect, not fleeting attention. Authentic respect endures beyond transient admiration. Redirect your focus inward; be your own staunchest ally. The individual unbound by the need for validation is the epitome of strength. By the grace of Christ Jesus, I stand amidst the remnants of my former self, a testament to resilience. I rise from the ashes, empowered by the permission I granted myself. My destiny was always one of brilliance; though shrouded in darkness by others in my youth, I now shine brightly, guided by divine purpose. My life is a canvas, painted by the hand of God; alone, I am nothing. I commit to toil until my achievements rival the magnitude of a phone number. It's not about appearances; it's about substance. When aspirations eclipse revelry, welcome to the elite 1% club.

A dream, inscribed with a date, transforms into a goal.

A goal, dissected into actions, evolves into a plan.

A plan, executed with resolve, manifests into reality.

Nothing's out of reach if you dedicate daily time to your aspirations. You've got the power to make it a reality. Don't hold yourself back—keep moving forward! The key is to rise after every fall, whether you're running, walking, or crawling. Know that God will see you through it all. 85% of folks have had a dream so vivid, they weren't sure if it'd materialize. The remaining 15% turn dreams into reality. Mine have, and I'm living them to the fullest. I didn't wait on others; I refused to give up. I put in the work, and now I'm reaping the rewards! I wish there were two of me—I could use the extra help sometimes, haha! By changing my habits, my life changed for the better. Now, I treat myself to solo dates, explore new places, and surround myself with positive energy. I celebrate my progress and achievements, even if no one else knows about them! If you can comfortably dine or catch a movie solo, you can tackle anything life throws your way. I'm unafraid to venture into uncharted territory; I'm becoming the person I was meant to be.

God has a purpose for my journey, and it's to prepare me for what I've prayed for. He told me to lay my troubles at his feet, and He'd handle them. So, I did, and He's coming through, just as He promised. I'm not a Christian because I'm flawless; I'm a Christian because I recognize my weakness and need for a savior. He's got me better than I have myself.

I don't need fancy clothes or a partner to feel confident.

My honesty is my beauty. I

'm intelligent, courageous, self-assured, compassionate, independent, strong, and graceful.

I am chosen!

My life is continually improving because I've done the internal work and will keep doing so for my growth. I began by forgiving myself for prioritizing others' happiness over my own. Now, I ensure my own happiness comes first. The future holds more significance than the past. I'm honoring and celebrating myself! Never downplay your blessings to appease others. God blessed you intentionally! You deserve the same love you give to others. Know your worth!

Ask yourself honestly, have you acknowledged your private accomplishments?

When you find joy in something privately, there's no need to flaunt it on social media. I march to the beat of my own drum. I don't engage in competition with others. I carve out my own path and follow my own lead. I'm committed to staying true to my principles until divine intervention manifests something real. Comparing myself to others doesn't make me; I recognize my uniqueness on a spiritual level. As it's said, comparison steals joy (2 Corinthians 10:12).

One thing I truly cherish about myself is that despite any mistreatment or adversity I face, my heart remains pure, brimming with boundless love to share. That's a part of me no one can tarnish. There's no need to seek external validation to love oneself. Some may still dwell on my past self, unaware of the transformation I've undergone. Though I possess the ability to strike with my words, I opt for humility, counting my blessings while leaving judgment to a God. That's what I call grace. Exuding silent strength, coupled with inner laughter, holds a unique power. I choose to treat others not as they are, but as I am—worthy of kindness.

In essence, I've distanced myself from negative influences altogether. It's imperative not to be one's own worst enemy, hindering personal growth. I refuse to compromise my standards for anyone; instead, I inspire them to rise to my level. Self-respect empowers me. I safeguard my peace by reciprocating effort where it's genuinely given. I found tranquility when I relinquished emotional burdens that weren't mine to carry. Absorbing others' trauma and projections is no longer part of my journey. I deserve genuine companionship, individuals who nurture my soul, well-being, and essence.

It's crucial to remember that selfish individuals prioritize their own interests, only valuing you when you serve their agenda. In my youth, I admired those with material luxuries, but now, I esteem those with inner peace, much like myself. True character shines brightest in the shadows, where actions speak louder than words, away from prying eyes and judgment.

What used to trip me up, I now stride over effortlessly.

If you knew the struggle and time it took to rebuild my peace and happiness, you'd understand why I'm so discerning about who I let into my life or my space. Surround yourself with those who uplift and inspire you, not those who drain your energy. Once someone shows their true colors through toxic behavior, they can't expect me to see them any differently.

People may hurl insults when they can't manipulate you. Before engaging in conflict, consider whether the other person is mature enough to comprehend differing viewpoints. If not, it's futile. Refrain from depleting yourself trying to rescue everyone around you. Self-care is paramount. I refuse to engage in arguments; my mental well-being takes precedence over bruised egos. By remaining silent, I emerge victorious.

Don't settle for a mundane existence; aspire to soar like an eagle, not chatter aimlessly like a parrot. Parrots may talk incessantly but lack the ability to soar. Eagles, on the other hand, maintain silence and possess the power to touch the sky. Beware of those with empty heads and verbose mouths. People gossip behind your back for three reasons:

1. When they feel inferior to you.

2. When they covet what you possess.

3. When they attempt to emulate your lifestyle but fall short.

Other people's opinions of you? That's their issue, not yours. You're in control of not letting others affect you emotionally, mentally, or spiritually. They can't hurt you if you don't hand them the ammunition. I used to give certain folks a second chance to take a shot at me because they missed the mark the first time! But that girl? She's gone, vanished, never to resurface again. Nowadays, you can't afford to give folks the benefit of the doubt. They are who they show you they are.

You could lay down like a doormat, and people would still find fault with your flatness! Love yourself enough to recognize when you're being mistreated and move on. As we grow, we realize it's more important to have real friends than a bunch of acquaintances. Rudeness is often a sign of someone's own unhappiness. Wish them well and keep it moving.

Don't lose yourself trying to please someone else, no matter who they are. Be your own best friend. Be everything you need for yourself. You're special too! Be your own hero; sometimes, you've got to isolate yourself to stay focused— that's called discipline. Don't go back to people who repeatedly hurt you; that's disrespecting yourself. Monsters are real, and they look like regular people.

Missing someone isn't an excuse to jump back into a toxic situation. Believe that everything happens for a reason. People change, and sometimes it's so you can learn to let go. Things fall apart to make room for better things. Don't force connections with folks who don't see your worth.

I'm too blessed to stoop to anyone's level. I can't afford—or want—the bad karma. Weak people seek revenge; strong people forgive; smart people walk away. I stopped explaining how I should be treated; I just started walking away, blocking, and keeping my distance. And you know what? My life's been peaceful.

I'm not afraid of being alone; I fear being around people I can't trust. I vibe with those I can trust blindly. My time is precious; I won't waste it on trivial people or things. I've been through too much to let anyone hurt me again. Expectations lead to disappointment. People won't always move, think, or act like you do.

Just because people lose me as a friend or family member doesn't mean they've gained an enemy. I still want them to eat, just not at my table. Before getting upset, ask yourself if it's worth wasting your time being angry. Everyone deserves a second chance, but not for the same mistake. Actions not aligning with words? That's manipulation. Refusing to take responsibility? That's gaslighting. Know when to cut ties with both.

I'll always be a "problem" because I won't let people walk all over me.

Anything beyond your control is a lesson in growth. Don't fret over who might take offense if you speak your truth; worry about those who may be misled, deceived, or harmed if you don't. Be authentic, express yourself, for those who truly matter won't judge, and those who judge don't matter! We're all flawed; we stumble, we err, we fall, but we also rise, learn, evolve, and press on, grateful for the chance to make things right.

When someone feels threatened by you, it's not you they fear—it's your success that intimidates them. Failure isn't a setback; it's a stepping stone to growth. If you're afraid to fail, you'll never progress. Swallow your pride, embrace failure as a means of progress, and strive for success.

I can't let killers kill my self-esteem

I use my prayers and my energy to power my dreams

The devil tried to kill me, but I looked to the stars,

I prayed to the lord, and he gave me the stars

He healed all my wounds and cleared all my scars!

The end will always tell,

I am who I am on purpose and without

Your permission.

Written by me

Your favorite author

L.spikes

It had to be me. I was chosen for this path.

Seek maturity, loyalty, stability, and peace, not mere appearances. True beauty lies within, and as one matures, they understand the power of silence over proving a point. Once you've made your point, let it be. Maturity is when you choose understanding over retaliation when someone wrongs you. My journey has taught me that while hurt may shape me, it does not define me. In moments of chaos, remember, sometimes things are falling into place rather than apart. Emerging from life's storms transforms you irrevocably. That's the essence of the storm; embrace it. The future holds greatness in store, courtesy of the divine power of God.

Envision the possibilities if you weren't constrained by insecurities. Allow your imagination to lead the way, visualize your aspirations vividly. Those who navigate life solo possess the strongest resilience. Don't let emotions dictate your decisions; pause and seek guidance through prayer. God's intervention can alter everything. A departure from routine often proves beneficial. Change may be daunting, yet stagnation is equally fearsome. You're not trapped; rather, you're entrenched in familiar patterns that once served you. However, these behaviors now hinder rather than help. To progress, adopt a new approach, perhaps through prayer. You never know the outcome until you try. Standing firm in your beliefs amidst a world accustomed to settling signifies strength.

Determine the life you desire and document your aspirations. Fun fact: writing is akin to thinking, and God hears our thoughts. Hence, my daily journaling habit. Refuse anything that contradicts the life you envision, including substances. Release what doesn't align with your aspirations. Be resolute in your decisions. I embody this strength. Thank you, Jesus.

Eccedentesiast: someone who masks their pain with a smile. Were you once that person? I was. I granted myself forgiveness for tolerating and accepting things I shouldn't have. I confronted my past self, forgave her, and resolved to no longer conceal my pain. You can do the same. Fear only amplifies if left unaddressed.

When you become immune to the opinions and actions of others, you shield yourself from needless suffering. What others think of you is really none of your concern, and life becomes much simpler that way. If someone takes issue with you but talks about it to everyone except you, it's not about you—it's about their craving for attention.

They may have laughed at me because I was different, but now I chuckle at their sameness. I've learned to see past the facade and seek the authenticity in people because genuine goodness is often concealed by a facade. Authenticity is unadorned and unashamed, regardless of the scars it bears. I've come to love everyone and trust that God will sort them out in due time.

The longer you entertain what doesn't belong to you, the more you delay what does. One day, it will all make sense. You'll discern what truly matters and what doesn't. You'll care less about others' opinions of you and more about how you view yourself. Take stock of how far you've come and recall when you thought things were irreparable—then smile. Smile because you're genuinely proud of yourself and the person you've fought to become. Material possessions hold no significance; it's your character that defines you. Take a closer look at yourself. Instead of asking why something is happening, ask yourself what it's teaching you. God doesn't always communicate in black and white; sometimes, you must decipher the lessons hidden between the lines and recognize that everything happens for a reason.

At my lowest point, all I had was God, and I clung to Him for dear life. And now? I am a daughter of the King of Kings! I walk as such—unmoved by the world's wickedness. I speak as such—God and Christ ever present on my lips. I dress as such—fully armored. I am not who I once was. I've been redirected from the highway to hell to the pathway to heaven.

I will ascend to my greatest heights in Christ! I cherish who I have become and who I am becoming. I have no time or energy for hate. Loving others, wishing them well, or praying for their healing is where I invest my energy. God saved me to reveal my own greatness. Here I am, sharing life lessons from my own journey to aid you. God, help me so I can help you!

I am that person who roots for others, who encourages them to believe in themselves and their dreams, just as I'm doing for you as you read this transformative book. The most valuable possession you can have in this day and age is peace of mind. Don't let anyone rob you of that! Reflect on these thoughts and questions each week, and assess your personal growth:

1. I feel

2. I need

3. I Forgive/forgave

4. I celebrate

5. I release

6. I trust God

Some things are beyond your control like other people's feelings, behaviors, actions, words, and thoughts. But you do have control over your own thoughts, words, actions, and behaviors, as well as how you choose to respond to others. Sometimes, no matter how kind, caring, or loving you are, it's simply not enough for some people. We end relationships with those we love, not because we want to, but because we know we deserve better.

I've grown comfortable with my own company. I've learned to be okay with not always being invited, included, or considered. After a while, I realized I wasn't missing out on anything anyway. Don't chase after people—if they enjoy spending time with you, they'll make the effort. If not, be content in your own company.

It's time to make people understand that it's a privilege to be a part of your life. I'm loyal, but once I sense that I'm unwanted, I leave people to those they hold in higher regard. It may be tough, but for the sake of your self-respect, it's necessary. You'll be okay—trust in God. And know your worth. If you don't recognize your own value, don't expect others to do it for you.

All relationships thrive on respect, honesty, support, trust, and accountability. However, some relationships are meant to teach you to walk away from what no longer serves you. When people underestimate you, let your positive actions and results speak volumes. Be so content in who you are that others' actions no longer shake you.

If you want to understand someone, listen to their words; if you want to know their heart, observe their actions. As you strive for excellence in your life, be prepared to lose some people along the way. Pursuing greatness can make others uncomfortable, but that's your journey to navigate.

Don't fret if not everyone likes you—many people struggle to even like themselves. Learn to see people for who they truly are and place them accordingly in your life. You are the CEO of your own life—hire, fire, and promote accordingly. Life becomes simpler when you stop seeking love from monsters who carry their own demons.

People would learn from their mistakes if they weren't so busy denying them. It takes humility to admit when you've made a mistake. Some people may lose you simply by entertaining the thought of ignoring or neglecting you. Everything happens because God allows it—trust in His divine wisdom.

When faced with hurt, pain, or unfairness, you have a choice: to hold onto the banner of victimhood or to embrace victory. You can't hold both at the same time.

Which banner do you hoist, or will you? And why? Jot it down and recite it daily.

The silver lining of tough times? You see everyone's true colors.

Character defines you. Reputation? It's just what folks think of you.

I've weathered too many storms to let a few raindrops faze me, in a world where nobody gives a damn. I don't air my grievances, making them fester. I surrender them to God and keep forging ahead.

Mental fortitude equals staying serene, joyful, and effective regardless of the circumstances. My personality throws folks off. I relish solitude, yet I'm quite the social butterfly. My surroundings shape my demeanor—I can be boisterous or subdued, depending on the vibe. I read the room and adapt. Sometimes I'm up for a party, other times I just crave my own company.

Smile, because the world doesn't revolve around your problems! Smiling suits me! Smiles are infectious! It's a shame some folks resent seeing you grin, especially when you're genuinely happy! No one can rob me of my smile! Your mind believes whatever you feed it—so feed it love! Don't let your fears push you around. Follow the dreams in your heart, not the fears in your mind. For instance, talk more about your blessings than your burdens. People tend to dwell on their pain and suffering rather than their joy and contentment. I've shifted from griping to celebrating.

Let me ask you: when was the last time you felt genuine joy? (Honestly!)

God's spirit bestows joy independent of our circumstances! Grant yourself the freedom to live large, stop playing small! You're destined for greatness. Satan might tarnish beauty, but God turns ruins into something beautiful! I'm a living testament to that! Trust your journey, even when it baffles you. Testimonies serve to humiliate the devil! Silence is what the devil craves; he doesn't want folks singing God's praises! Be discerning, be shrewd, never get so desperate that you drink from any cup handed to you. Your mind is a garden, your thoughts are the seeds—choose whether to grow flowers or weeds. Remember: when they underestimate you, when they mistake your kindness for weakness, when they exploit your gentleness, you rise and show them what hell looks like on a gentle human

You've got to do this for yourself. This is your journey. It's not about anyone else. Live for yourself. Honor yourself. Never lose sight of that! Settling for less than you deserve yields nothing but disappointment. Stop berating yourself for what you lack and start adoring yourself for what you already possess. Sometimes the worst things that happen lead us straight to the best things yet to come! If you're going through a rough patch, stay positive and pray harder. You can never pray too much.

God always has three responses to our prayers:

1. "Yes, I will bless you. You've fulfilled my requirements."

2. "Yes, but not yet. There are lessons I need to impart."

3. "No, I have a better plan for you. Trust me with your life."

Remain grateful for what is to come. Everything I prayed for will manifest abundantly! Keep praying, remain patient. God is orchestrating everything for your benefit. God's love is unconditional, and He grants us free will to choose Him. God is easy!

Prayer to Read Out Loud

"Search me, O God, and know my heart; test me and know my anxious thoughts. See if there is any offensive way in me, and lead me in the way everlasting.**" (Psalm 139:23-24)**

This prayer is for you, dear reader: Prayer to Read Out Loud

Dear God, I humbly kneel before you. Illuminate the darkness within me, strengthen my weaknesses, mend what is broken, heal what is ailing, and reignite any peace and love that has faded within me. In Jesus' name, Amen.

You can recite this prayer daily upon awakening and before retiring for the night.

When you're fed up with being tired of the same old, you'll put a stop to many things. I reached my breaking point and stopped tolerating a lot of negativity. It transformed me into a better person. I refuse to allow negative influences in my life while I'm on the path to success.

As I age, my tolerance for drama, conflict, and stress diminishes. I seek the company of happy people, engaging in positive activities, and purposefully enjoying life.

"I will run and not grow weary; I will walk and not be faint." You can bounce back from any setback with the right mindset. Don't allow anyone to limit your potential. You may stumble temporarily, but a resilient individual will always rise, rebuild, and return stronger than ever. I am a testament to this truth.

Some of us never find happiness because we're too busy pretending. God blesses those who endure trials and temptations, promising them the crown of life. James 1:12

Every day is a chance to align ourselves with God's will. Don't let doubt deter you. With Christ's strength, you can overcome any obstacle. I am grateful to both God and Christ, who shower me with blessings and allow me to approach them with my desires.

God has a purpose for each of us. Rise up and reclaim the life stolen by the enemy. Share your testimony of God's goodness, for His blessings are meant to be shared for His glory.

Keep this in mind: when God is gearing to elevate you, chaos will ensue. You'll feel let down by people, even those closest to you; family and friends may betray you, leaving you to stand alone in that moment, with only God as your anchor. But remember, nothing occurs without His consent. No one can harm you unless He permits it. He's pulling the strings, whether you realize it or not. Your current circumstances are a direct result of past. Always be prepared to weather the storm alone. People can change in the blink of an eye. Today, you may be significant to them, but tomorrow, you might mean nothing. That's just the harsh reality of life. This life-changing book is in your hands, urging you to start making better decisions for better outcomes. When you're done reading, tell the devil he can go to the place that awaits him. Claim the life God has ordained for you since the day you were born.

Back when I was lost, living a worldly existence, unsure of my identity, I turned to marijuana, alcohol, the wrong crowd, and adorned my body with tattoos. After years of living according to the devil's playbook, I turned my life over to Christ and decided to pursue education. I realized that exercising my mind and placing my faith in God far outweighed any temporary fixes. Today, I stand as a formidable woman, empowered in every aspect of my life. I've diversified my skill set: I am a certified carpenter (and currently work as an administrative assistant in the field), become a trained chef (which led to owning my own catering business, albeit temporarily on hold as I explore new ventures), attained a diploma as a medical office specialist (enabling me to manage both front and back office duties alongside physicians), and soon, I'll add professional nail technician to my repertoire (having honed my skills over five years). In addition, I'm on the brink of becoming a best-selling author with this transformative book, slated for release soon.

My message to the world is simple: merely existing isn't living. Longevity surpasses fleeting pleasures. I am living proof that a saint is simply a sinner who chose to rise again.

You might be grappling with challenges, unsure how to achieve your dreams. But trust me, God has it all mapped out; just have faith, and you'll be alright. We may stumble, love the wrong things, shed tears over the wrong reasons, but every mistake guides us closer to the right path. Don't forget to prioritize yourself now—it's not selfish; it's essential.

An investment in knowledge yields the best returns. I've got smarts aplenty, courtesy of God granting me wisdom and insight. Before anything else, I belong to the God. I'm a unique kind of beauty. Never doubt your worth for anyone else; always question if they're worthy of you.

Things you shouldn't apologize for:

1. Being ambitious

2. Needing a break

3. Asking for help

4. Setting boundaries

5. Having emotions

Repeat - I lack nothing. I have the tools necessary to succeed in every area of my life. I am capable, resilient, and intelligent. <u>I cannot lose</u>. I'm in the perfect position to get there from here and to take all the steps i deem necessary in order to reach my goals.

Remember, you already possess the power to do, be, or create anything you desire. **Psalm 37:7-8**

Chapter 14:
Overcoming Obstacles on the Path to Self-Realization

Pushing Forward: Defying All Odds to Reach My Higher Self

You can't win in life if you're losing in your mind. Change your thoughts, and you'll transform your life. Mental toughness isn't about having a full tank; it's finding fuel even when it seems empty. Remember, a negative mindset will never yield a positive life. So, nourish your mind with positivity, and watch as great things start gravitating towards you.

We're constantly reminded to stay positive, yet negativity often seeps through the cracks. Train your mind to perceive the positive in every situation and witness a profound difference. Each morning, set out to surpass yesterday's self, and you'll end the day feeling fulfilled and accomplished. There's always room for improvement, so whatever you tackle today, push yourself, and you'll triumph!

Never apologize for embracing your awesomeness! A leader's mission is to make a difference—it's about the goal, not the role. Remember, nothing is insurmountable if you dedicate yourself daily to your aspirations. Be productive, not merely busy. And when something truly aligns with your path, you won't need to force it; it will unfold naturally. Don't let a setback provoke the worst in you. Instead, remember this: whoever you are, your soul exudes brilliance. Stop regretting your kindness; those who encountered you needed your light. Stay committed to love, and the beauty of your truth will radiate effortlessly.

Confidence isn't about superiority over others; it's the absence of the need for external validation. I'm confident in myself; I don't seek validation, which empowers me profoundly. Sometimes, when you feel buried in the depths of darkness, in reality, you're being planted, and all seeds flourish in the dirt.

Here I stand, resilient and steadfast, a testament to resilience. My scars narrate tales of resilience; they remind me of when life attempted to shatter me and failed. For those facing unfair trials, know this: God promises restoration and abundance beyond measure. Even when you feel depleted, there's strength within you; keep fighting! To you, silently battling your demons, I am sending love to you and remember, you don't owe the world an explanation for your struggles. Live authentically without the need to showcase every high or low. Some doors close to propel you forward; trust in God's timing and relinquish control. Embrace the journey, for it's astounding where faith can lead when you trust in God.

People may exit your life unexpectedly but trust that God's plan is greater. No adversary can prevail when God is on your side. I thank God for protecting me from what I thought I wanted and blessing me with what I truly needed. You are fearfully and wonderfully made; awaken your inner strength—it's time to conquer! For those who emerged from adversity, know this: you're destined for greatness. Embrace your past mistakes; they sculpted the resilient individual you are today. Remember, it's not about winning or losing; it's about learning and growing. Don't fear failure; fear stagnation. Dare to pursue your aspirations, even if it scares you. Your resilience sets you apart; embrace your journey, for you were made to endure.

We're allotted limited chances to seize our desires. Nothing is more regrettable than squandering an opportunity that could alter your trajectory. So, stop fretting over trivial matters and reclaim your happiness. Embrace life's lessons, for they shape your resilience. Amidst turmoil, remember: even when you're not okay, you're still strong. Strong individuals may bend but never break; they rebuild and persevere. So, which will you choose—to break silently and rise or to remain shattered?

No one endures more trials and tribulations than a person with a good heart. Rest assured, God recognizes the purity within you, ensuring that things will always align in your favor. Trust me on this! If you're inclined to give, it's vital to set boundaries with the takers in your life. They have no limits and will take as long as you allow them to.

Don't carry shame for what you've been through; instead, take pride in conquering the monsters of your past and those yet to come. You've survived days you thought impossible, demonstrating immense bravery. It may not have been an easy journey, but you're here! It takes great courage to overcome the struggles you've faced. Keep pushing forward; you're doing remarkably well.

I've endured difficult times myself, and at my lowest, all I had was God. What didn't work out for me actually turned out for the best! Everything always falls into place better than we can imagine. I'm grateful to God for revealing people's true intentions, unmasked from the façade they wear for the public eye. People may speak pleasing words, but God always unveils their genuine motives. Sometimes, we must endure the worst to attain the best. Life is about balance—be kind, but don't allow others to abuse you in any form. Trust, but stay vigilant against deception. Be content, but never cease striving for self-improvement. *What are you doing today? Is it bringing you closer to where you want to be tomorrow?*

When you feel like you have nothing left, that's when you should push harder; the rewards will be greater and more appreciated because of the journey you've endured. I'm cheering you on! Handle your business! You can't build a reputation on what you're going to do; get it done! Take the risk or lose the chance. First, they will ignore you, then they will laugh at you, then they will fight you, and after that, you will win! Trust the process. Be who you want to be, not what other people want to see. Don't let others define you; stay true to yourself. Never stop being a good person, regardless of others' actions; God knows your heart. There will be painful moments in your life that will alter your world in a matter of minutes. Let these moments make you stronger, smarter, and kinder, but never lose sight of who you are. Cry, scream if you have to, straighten your crown and keep moving forward. Remember, nothing changes until you change. Utilize your gifts; we are all born with them, and they will always pave the way for you. Whether you think you can or can't, you're right. Understand that fear often stems from the unknown, but refuse to be afraid. As Psalm 56:3 says, *"Fear not,"* said the Lord. My help comes from God, and He has equipped me to share this life-changing, motivating, encouraging, and inspiring memoir based on the teachings He imparted to me.

Call me crazy, but I find joy in witnessing people happy and succeeding. Life is a journey, not a competition. Focus on your growth like a flower that blooms without comparing itself to others. True strength lies not in showcasing your power to others but in the battles fought silently within. I am loved, called, and chosen. I am abundant in every way and generous on every occasion. I am anointed, appointed, equipped, and enabled by the power of God/Jesus working mightily within me! No weapons formed against me shall prosper, and no enemy scheme against me will succeed. I live, breathe, and serve powerfully under the shelter of God Almighty Himself. I am one of the chosen ones! Remember, your character outweighs anything toxic said against you; those who truly know you, know you.

In today's world, life is replete with hurt and deceitful individuals. Be cautious of who you surround yourself with. I'm grateful for the past 25 years for revealing the true colors of those around me. Some may judge you for evolving, but others will celebrate your growth. Choose your circle wisely, as not everyone will be supportive of your positive changes; it may remind them of their own stagnancy. Understand the significance of focusing on self-improvement rather than projecting onto others. Reflecting on the past three years, I realize the transformative power of continual mental, emotional, and spiritual growth. I trust in God's plan, acknowledging His role in removing certain individuals from my life and guiding me on the right path. I've come to the realization that I am my own best friend; nobody supports me like God does. I advocate fiercely for myself and strive to be the best version of myself for those who truly deserve me.

Don't dwell on closed doors; new opportunities await those who keep moving forward. If you've read this far, I hope your mindset is shifting and your heart is receptive to the changes necessary for a bright future. Remember, your courage must surpass your fear, and your faith can move mountains while doubt can create obstacles. Don't merely exist; push yourself beyond your limits, for everything you desire lies beyond fear. Be scared and do it anyway

When you align your voice and body with your goals, you ignite a transformative energy. Embrace your missteps, for they pave the way for epic successes. Sometimes, the best course of action is to simply have faith that everything will work out for your betterment. God's timing is always perfect; trust in His plan. Never evaluate your worth through the eyes of those who fail to appreciate you. Set boundaries, prioritize self-love, and value your time and energy. Remember, you teach others how to treat you by establishing what you will and won't accept. As for my personal advice:

- Save money consistently, regardless of the amount.
- Master the skill of being comfortable alone and independent.
- Educate yourself continuously through reading.
- Prioritize your health and take care of your body.
- Love yourself first; don't wait for validation from others.

They tried it, but God protected me.

I am stalked daily by demons, yet angels guard me. I am heavenly protected! Every time I expose the truth about Satan's prophets, more try to come against me in the spiritual realm where darkness reigns. I speak the truth. There are countless witches, wizards, diviners, hypocrites, and enchanters in the world, misleading God's people. Those who practice evil magic, tarot cards, crystals, psychic readings, and witchcraft will face God's wrath continually.

To those reading this, God has a mission for you to complete according to your abilities, all for His glory. I thank God every day for choosing me out of this wicked world, allowing me to perceive things on a different level while remaining humble. Yes, God had to humble me, for like you, I, too, lived in the world before He called me! Now, I do what others won't so I can achieve what others can't, all for the glory of God, whose right hand is powerful.

You can't defeat your demons if you're still enjoying their company. All are called, but few are chosen. Be willing to become new, separate yourself from the world, turn your demons into art, your shadow into your friend, your fear into fuel, and your failures into teachers! Don't waste your pain; recycle your heart. Shout out to the pain that gave me understanding! Sometimes, we are tested not to reveal our weaknesses but to discover our strengths. Only God knows what we will have to endure to become whom He created us to be. Only God can open doors that no man can shut or try to keep closed. I thank God He has never allowed me to give up on my dreams that I am living and pursuing as I write this amazing book. My ideas are enhanced daily, my goals are set, and I accomplish them. My creativity improves with every use. Never stop improving yourself! If what you've been through has forged a warrior within you because you refuse to bow down to your demons, so be it! Let them deal with what they have created. *Psalm 37:9, be at peace with yourself and know your power*. No one is born a warrior; you choose to be one when you refuse to be seated when you refuse to back down, and when you stand up after getting knocked down.

If not you, then who? Consider this deeply. Never let the light within you die! The devil thinks he's slick with his tricks and the people he uses. He may lead you right to Jesus Christ, but when you find a better way of living, he'll get mad. Then he'll torment you, haunt you, trick you, and plot against you with his lies (which he is the father of), playing mind games with you. But remember, he walked Jesus Christ to the cross, not knowing that very move would always triumph over him in the spiritual realm and on earth! Now, he and his demons are attacking God's people on earth.

When you put on the full armor of God, you tell the devil he has to go through Jesus Christ to get to you! A warrior is a person who gets up despite all enemies trying to destroy them. A warrior declares victory before seeing it, believing they will receive miracles because they know the Lord they serve is alive and by their side. Every single person has to go through something that tries to destroy them so they can discover who they truly are. Some people are in your life to test you until you stand up and say: *"Enough is enough, I'm worth more than what you offer me."*

One day, I discovered my own light, my own inner warrior. I let my demons out to play, and they came back humbled by who I am without them. I snatched my power back, and the game changed. My inner demons are on my side now because the power in me comes with a light they will never overcome, so they no longer exist. I am now a mature and fully armored, super empathic warrior for the Lord. Ephesians 6:10. I am equipped with knowledge of how to fight against unseen enemies and win! I always carry the ace of spade (God) with me; the joker can't touch me. I call this chapter of my life untouchable and unstoppable! I'm spiritually leveled all the way up!

Everything evil someone has tried to do to me, God has already done to them. The wicked will be brought down by their own wickedness! It is written! I've transitioned into the Great Awakening. I'm royalty. I laugh without fear of the future. Proverbs 31:23. Pain travels through family lines until someone is ready to heal it in themselves. By going through the agony of healing, you no longer pass the poison chalice onto the generations that follow. This is an incredibly important and sacred work. God won't let me fail at this. I am the chosen one! When God delivers you from evil, do not keep in touch with it. The enemy only attacks you because you are valuable to God. Thieves don't break into empty houses. You are important! Make sure your lamp has oil, too, so you can see because the world is getting darker and darker. The devil operates in what you're fearful of. Stop giving him power over you, your mind, your life. He is a coward! God didn't give us a spirit of fear; no, He gave us power and a sound mind. The devil doesn't want you to discover your power over him in the name of Jesus Christ. Use the name of Jesus Christ in everything you say and do; the devil has no power over you! Understand how much power you will have in the name of Jesus Christ!

In a world plunged into darkness, would you be prepared to survive? Honestly, consider this question. Remember, darkness will never prevail over light in any way, shape, or form.

Don't allow negative energy to overpower the positive energy within you, which is unfortunately happening to many people in the world today. Demonic spirits are prevalent in these last days we are living in, but as a true warrior for Christ Jesus, you can overcome them.

I've seen demonic spirits in many people, and I've had to engage in spiritual warfare numerous times, even as I write this amazing book. The wicked have tried to come against me in the spiritual realm, but they only add to the stockpile of demonic spirits I've already bound and tied up. Most of these wicked individuals fear me now because they know the power within me will always triumph over their evil magic.

Through Christ who strengthens me, I have overcome all the monsters I've encountered in my life. I have endured attacks from witches, warlocks, evildoers, and more, but God has protected me every step of the way. Let me share a testimony to illustrate the power of God's protection. One morning, someone attempted to send a demonic spirit to harm me in the spiritual realm. However, the spirit they sent was already bound and twisted by God's power. This incident revealed the darkness within that person's heart and thoughts, but it also demonstrated the power of God working through me.

I trust God to keep me safe from all evil and harm with my full heart. I am always spiritually warfare-ready, and those who come against me with harmful intentions will know the power of Christ within me. God exposes the fakes, the liars, and the deceivers. People may try to destroy you, but they often end up destroying themselves. I thank God daily for being my protector and guide.

While the devil prepares the world for the anti-Christ, the Holy Spirit is preparing Jesus' followers for the rapture. So, stand strong in your faith, knowing that God's protection is always with you. Have you considered where you're headed on that coming day—Heaven or Hell? Reflect on the way you're living and what's in your heart.

"The benefits are enjoyed by the servants of the Lord; their vindication will come from me; I the Lord have spoken" (Isaiah 54:17). Those who have spoken against me will eat their own words—my God is my defender. God cuts off every branch that doesn't produce fruit and prunes those that do so that they will bear even more fruit (John 15:2). He always sets me up to win, regardless of those who wish me to lose.

People often underestimate the privilege of being part of someone's life until they find themselves on the outside trying to get back in. It's your character and how you treat others that determine your value. Disrespect is not tolerated—I stand firm on that. Now, I crave the freedom to live life on my own terms, aligned with my soul's purpose and life mission in Jesus' name.

"This I declare about the Lord your God: He alone is my refuge, my place of safety. He is my God, and I trust him for everything" (Psalm 91:2).

Let's embark on this journey together, drawing strength from the trials we've overcome. There will be moments when the weight of the world seems too heavy to bear, but remember: you've conquered mountains before, and you can do it again. On those days when doubt creeps in and whispers that you're not enough, silence it with the truth: you are resilient, capable, and destined for greatness. And when life throws its worst at you, hold fast to the belief that every storm eventually gives way to sunshine.

It was something I had to go through to be who I am spiritually today

I am the chosen one!

If you want to be successful, you have to be willing to disappear for a while. I am so comfortable with being alone because what I want, I don't need a crowd to get it. The size of your audience doesn't matter. Me being along was/is the upgrade. If the plat doesn't work, change the plan never the goal!

Are your habits getting you closer to achieving your goals or holding you back? (honestly)

Motivation is what gets you started; habits is what keeps you going. Focus on your goal. Don't look in any other direction but ahead. Showing you results are more effective than telling your plan! It's never about who has more talent, it's about who is hungrier and being okay if it happens and okay if it doesn't! Which is a very powerful place to be. I'm just a woman who decided to go for it, because I wanted more out of life, than what I had been given! I deserve all that God has for me! Almost every successful person begins with two beliefs: the future can be better than the present, and knowing you have the power to make it happen. I turned out better than my family thought I would, being that I am my mom daughter. I'm sure *they all* spoke bad things over my life years ago, but God had/has/got his own plans for me. I'm an inspiration/motivation to others even the ones that hate me lol. Many let my success get to them, some distance themselves from me, some didn't say nothing, and strangers motivated me to keep going. As I look back, I had false supporters, and fake friendships. The people I needed support from at the time did not support me. I can even remember my little sister daisy wishing me luck at the same time saying, "you going to self-destruct" because I wouldn't let someone who tried to steal my get down, steal my get down! Lol. *Family!!* As I come to today in time all I can do is laugh, be happy, humble, grateful, thankful and continue to be a blessing and be blessed, because every day I get better and better. I'm self-improving to the top! My point is whether you believe you can or not you are right. Nurture your powers of self-belief and it will take you to wonderful places. A person who masters patience, masters everything else. You are what you think about. You become who you surround yourself with. I like being alone. I have control over my own stuff. Therefore, in order to win me over, your presence has to feel better than my solitude. You're not competing with another person; you are competing with my comfort zones. There is nothing I enjoy more than minding my own business, finding new ways to grow, and making moves in silence. You say antisocial, I say at peace! The older I get, the more I understand that some people will stay the same and I do not have to be the fixer. Funny thing about getting older, your eyesight may weaken yet you can see through people much better. Make sure everybody in your boat is rowing instead of punching holes, being jealous, and envious while plotting on your normal life. Leo's don't know how to stop, which can lead to a lot of success but also a few disasters too. I had to stop watering the dead plants that surrounded me because they refused to grow. If you're not growing you are *dying!* I had to let them wither away and water my own plants with wisdom, understanding, knowledge, growth, and intelligence. If you have told the wicked person(s) and they do not turn from their evil ways, *they will die for/in their sins*; but you will have saved yourself Ezekiel 3:19. I've never chosen the woman I was my path chose me instead. I have been many women in my life. The *provider* and *protector,* the *lover* and *fighter* and more. I wear many hats! The woman I value the most will always be the *survivor* and *warrior*. I have fought the good fight. I have finished the race. I have kept the faith. 2 Timothy 4:7. I didn't need anyone slowing me down so I created my own lane! I was ready to vibrate higher and become a magnet of miracles. Now I'm in this place where everything feels right, my heart is calm, my soul is lit, my vision is clear. Life is too short to tolerate nonsense. I am at peace with where I've been and at peace with where I'm headed! Nobody glows more than a person who finally *let that hurt go*! My insides are sparkles and glitter! I am at peace because I know God fight for me day and night. Heaven holds great conversations about me and my personal assigned angels are always near me ready to aid and assist me in all that I ask of them. I have lion blood and lion's bones; *I walk this earth filled with wicked people alone,* cowards run in packs. I will *never* eat with hyenas! Don't expect me too! *I've always love the idea of not being what people expect me to be, and outgrow the box they always trying to put me in.* I will always surpass one's expectation of me. I've learned to fly light extra baggage slow you down.

A plane can't land on a crowded runway. My setbacks was a blessing and might have amused some people and made them feel good about themselves, God had to slow things down because of the evil around me. I survived what was meant to destroy me. I came back like a boss, fabulous, wiser, and stronger than ever! My delays was *my protection* but my comeback is my resurrection! This is only the beginning. There are no breaks when you have goal and dreams for yourself. That seed that was planted in the dirt has flourished and is blooming right now lol! Always make sure you have the last laugh no matter how long it take. People will take you for granted and God will show them that you were/are rare, their lost! There will come a time in your life when people regret why they treated you wrong. Trust me, it will definitely come. Every person has lost that one loyal person just because that loyal person was so loyal, that person thought the loyal person would never leave! Again, their lost! I was assigned this mountain to show other that it can be moved. I trusted the process, I pushed harder, and I won! Every day is another chance to change your life. Don't judge yourself with others because you are different from them. Focus less on what you are going through, set your eyes on where God is leading you, keep going, if you stumble and fall rise up, and try again. Do not lose hope, please believe there are a thousand beautiful things waiting for you. Sunshine comes to all those who feels rain. Promise yourself to be strong, that nothing can disturb your peace of mind. Intelligence is beauty. Intelligent people tend to care less about the opinions of others, they also enjoy being alone to protect their peace. Work on yourself and vibe alone is the best way to win! You don't need company every season. Don't rely on anyone but yourself. Never give up on something you really want. A part of being strong is learning how to fight alone. The pain will go away, the tears will dry up. It's just a matter of time, be proud of yourself for how hard you're trying. Things will change for you when you just do it. The same success, love, money, happiness, time, energy, and peace is available to everyone, kids or not. You can turn those 24 hours that are available to you into the life you always dreamed of.

Will you?

Let me be your motivation, inspiration, and encouragement. If I can do it after going through what I been through you can too! Let's do it together. There will be days when you feel like giving up, but don't. There will be days when you feel like you just don't have what it takes, but you do! There will be days when everything seems to be falling apart but it won't! You must know things will work out for the good and there will be days that you look back and say I am glad I never gave up! Or you may be glad God never gave up on you. When you feel like you are drowning in life, don't worry your lifeguard walks on water.

"I shall run and not be weary; I shall run and not faint." - Isaiah 40:31

Keep pressing forward, knowing that every step you take brings you closer to victory. Together, we'll conquer the challenges that lie ahead and emerge stronger than ever before.

Testimony… I did a 264 hour (I'll let you total the days) miracles fast of consuming no food of any sort! (I only drank the protein naked juices) if I never see one again it will be too soon lol! But my God told me to do so. I was also smoking black and mild cigars. This fast was to stop me from smoking.

I tell you at the end of my 264 hours, I felt super naturally powerful. Not once did I feel a hunger pain, not once did my stomach growl, not once did I get a headache, not once did I feel weak, not once did I faint, not once!!! But every day I looked for those things to happen and *not once did they come to me.*

In my 264th hour I felt like I could go another week but my God had told me to eat. In my 216th hour, I had no desire to smoke, *I haven't smoked since.* I also lost 11 pounds during my miracle fast. I knew it was just me and God. I kept it to myself until I had completed the days, he wanted me too. I was so proud of myself. I had never gone long as I had without eating anything. In my 216th hour it got a little harder because I was coming to the end of it. I was tempted to eat before I completed my 264 hours.

It seemed like food was just calling me. I felt weak to the temptation but I had something to prove to God and myself and I did it. I prayed and prayed for God to give me the strength mentally, emotionally, and physically to complete my 264 hour fast. Those hours were specifically my goal, nothing more nothing less.

When I had completed my 264 hours fast, I didn't have the taste for the things I had before I started fasting. Everything sweet didn't taste sweet, it had a nasty taste to it. I was wasting money on things that I didn't want or couldn't eat anymore, because they did not meet my taste bud on my palate. God had changed my eating habits during my miracle fast so, not only did I stop smoking but I started eating different too, and not by my own doing, but by God's doing for he knows what's best for me and you! God blesses those who patiently endures testing and temptation. Afterwards they will receive the crown of life that God has promised those who love Him. James 1:12

The undisciplined person remains enslaved to their weaknesses, but discipline sets us free. Lasting success is attainable with it. Discipline isn't merely a choice; it's a collection of powerful habits ingrained into our daily lives. My dreams outweigh my need for sleep. Each morning, I awaken with a fervent desire to make every moment count, a commitment to productivity that honors the time granted by God.

In Romans 12:1, we're urged to offer our bodies as living sacrifices, holy and pleasing to God—a true act of worship. Trusting in God and Jesus Christ fills me with courage, even in moments of uncertainty (Psalm 56:3).

Brothers and sisters, when troubles arise, embrace them as opportunities for growth and joy. Monitor your thoughts and actions, ensuring they align with the life you aspire to lead. Cultivate a mindset that invites God and Jesus to work in your favor, for a shift in perspective can yield profound change. Embrace the journey, for even the darkest chapters will one day become powerful parts of your testimony. Surround yourself with those who uplift, inspire, and love unconditionally.

Integrity is doing the right thing even when no one is watching

I woke up one morning and asked myself, what is life about? I found the answers in my room. The ac said, "be cool you can adjust." The ceiling said, "aim high reach for the sky." The window said "see the world! It's a beautiful painting." The time on my phone said "make the most of every minute, time don't wait on no one." The mirror on my wall said, "focus on yourself not others, be productive." The calendar said, "stay updated on your goals and dreams." The door said, "only God can open and shut me for you, pusher harder for what you want." The floor said "at God's feet is where you leave everything and trust him to take care of it for you. Never except no for an answer when you know what you desire is God's will for you.

I firmly believe that the latter half of life holds the promise of greater joy and fulfilment. The first half may be dedicated to discovering how to navigate life's challenges, but the second half is about relishing in its abundance. I find myself living the most vibrant years of my life now. Remember, just because the past didn't unfold as planned, it doesn't dictate the potential of your future. Your best days may be yet to come, surpassing even your wildest dreams. To the firstborns, I offer this blessing: may your pockets never run dry. As assistant parents, you carry a unique burden and responsibility. May God grant you financial empowerment to fulfil your duties with grace.

Let's not overlook the resilience and strength found in those labelled as damaged souls or black sheep. Listen to me when I sat it's those damaged souls, the black sheep, the ones that grew up too fast when reality hit them hard at a young age, the ones that knew pain and broken hearts for the first moment they could recall their thoughts, the ones that can struggle through anything life throws at them, because it's all they've ever known. It's the people that don't fit in in anywhere but know everybody. Those are the deepest, purest people you will ever encounter. I'm not saying this because I am one of those super dope people, but because it is truth!

- Good people bring happiness
- Bad people provide experiences
- Worst people teach us invaluable lessons.
- Best people gift us cherished memories that last a lifetime

If our standing in life depended solely on our moral compass, behavior, and treatment of others, how would we fare? God has already taken into account your wrong turns and mistakes; it's time to accept His mercy and move forward without dwelling on past shortcomings. Despite attempts to imitate or undermine, no one can replicate the essence of who we are. They may try to mimic your style, but true creativity is impossible to duplicate. People envy only reveals their own insecurities and unhappiness.

Jealousy and envy stem from insecurity and fear, traits that set you apart from those who seek to diminish you. While they may perceive you as a threat, remain focused on your own journey, striving to improve each day without comparison or competition. I'm not here to compete with anyone; I'm simply dedicated to becoming a better version of myself. Despite anyone's efforts to derail me, I'm determined and unwavering on my path. I'm not just here for the moment; I'm here to make a lasting impact. And in the end, it's God who will have the final say. Many have tried countless times to impede my progress, but I'm steadfast and resolute. I'm here to stay, and that's all there is to it.

I am the chosen one!

I am constantly amazed by how God reveals the truth to me, allowing me to see what others cannot. Through His guidance, I discern the true nature of individuals and uncover the falsehoods they may conceal. Testing spirits has become a habit, enabling me to recognize the presence of jealousy, envy, competition, and comparison—the hallmarks of Satan's influence.

Despite the prevalence of wickedness in the world, God's sovereignty remains unshaken. He exposes the schemes of the devil and his followers, ensuring that I am not led astray. In these tumultuous times, it's essential to remain vigilant and discerning, for evil often masquerades as light. No matter the challenges we face or the evil we encounter, nothing can thwart God's plans for us. He controls the times and seasons, elevating and deposing kings according to His will. As Daniel 2:21 states, it is God who imparts wisdom and understanding, guiding us through the darkness with His divine light.

While it may seem as though the devil holds sway over the world, prophecy is being fulfilled, and God's ultimate victory is assured. I urge everyone to educate themselves on the prophecies outlined in the Book of Revelation, for therein lies wisdom and clarity in these uncertain times. Forget the past, but remember its lessons, value clarity. Be open, honest, and transparent about your feelings and desires. Refuse to engage in guessing games when it comes to understanding someone's intentions or feelings towards you. You deserve the respect of straightforward communication, allowing you to make informed decisions that benefit your growth and well-being.

Reject the misconception that loudness equates to strength or that quietness signifies weakness. As an empath, I possess the ability to discern meaning beyond mere words—I listen to tone, observe body language, and interpret subtle cues that reveal the truth. Silence speaks volumes, and I can hear everything someone do not say in words. I pay attention to every nuance, ensuring I understand the full spectrum of communication.

I am not just a passive observer; I am an empath, attuned to the emotions and energies of those around me. This sensitivity is not a weakness but a source of power—a superpower if you will. Like the silent strength of a lion, I approach life with purpose and precision, understanding the significance of every action and decision. Excuse me while I carve out my path to success, guided by my intuition and empowered by my empathic abilities.

Chapter 15:
Divine Favor

Blessed beyond measure, highly favored, and divinely protected.

Covered by the hand of God, I've walked a path that defies the odds. From a young age, I faced demonic dreams and encounters, struggling to understand their significance. Yet, with time, I realized these experiences were part of a greater plan, shaping me into the warrior I am today. Throughout my life, God has granted me glimpses of the future, revealing His divine purpose piece by piece. Each revelation leaves me in awe, prompting me to seek further understanding. Some answers come quickly, while others require patience and trust in God's timing. Describing these encounters may seem unbelievable to some, even to my own children, who have witnessed God's power working through me. Initially, it unsettled them, but now they grasp the depth of my relationship with God and the extraordinary path I walk.

In Christ, I've found strength and purpose beyond measure. As I continue on this journey, I remain open to God's guidance, knowing His hands are firmly upon my life, guiding me through every challenge and triumph. With newfound clarity, I walk confidently in my light, pursuing my soul's purpose and life mission. When I say "I'm blessed," I don't mean money or material things. I mean situations that were sent to destroy me as a child or make me lose my mind as an adult but didn't even touch my soul type of blessed

Throughout my tumultuous journey. Even as a teenager growing up lost in the world, even as an adult trying to raise my children, even while I was living in the world being, doing, and thinking like the devil wanted me too —— God's hands have guided me, even when I strayed from His path. Now, more than ever, I stand firm in my identity and purpose, much to the devil's dismay. I am the chosen one, a warrior for Christ, unyielding in my faith and unafraid of death, for I know where my soul is bound. The vision of leaving this world, greeted by heavenly joy, fills me with anticipation, and I pray to see you there beside me.

The greatest miracle in my life is God's transformation of an unholy woman into a vessel of His holiness. He has placed me back into this world and kept me steadfast in His ways. As I pen this book, my prayer is that it guides you towards finding your own greatness beyond the pain and struggles. Fear no longer holds me captive, for I have conquered many monsters and emerged victorious. Just as you will, as you journey through these pages, discover God's purpose for your life. Know this: you were created for greatness, destined to shine and leave a mark on this world according to God's plan. Amidst the distractions and detours, stay focused on your divine purpose. I answer to no one but God, setting my own path and following His lead.

Falling in love with God has been my greatest blessing. I am His masterpiece, fearlessly standing before the devil as a child of God, a woman of faith, and a warrior for Christ Blessed, Highly Heavenly Protected. I owe everything to God, I lack nothing, for He provides abundantly. I trust in His timing and direction, knowing His blessings come when I need them most. My soul is precious, and I guard it against stress, envy, negativity, and deceit. My cup overflows with blessings, and I walk in the assurance that goodness and mercy will follow me all the days of my life.

Indeed, my cup overflows with blessings, as Psalm 23:5 declares. I've learned to expect goodness in my life because of my connection with God. I speak positivity into my life, trusting that God will bring it to fruition. I've broken the chains of generational curses, paving the way for blessings to flow to my children and future generations. Meeting Jesus as a Savior brings life, prosperity, and honor to those who pursue righteousness and love.

Every prayer is a testament to gratitude, not just a plea for needs. Trusting in God's listening ear, I pray about everything and worry about nothing, knowing He holds the power to add to my life in ways I cannot imagine. In these uncertain times, placing our trust in the Almighty is paramount. Only through Christ Jesus can we find salvation. Take a moment to reflect on your life and recognize the abundance of blessings bestowed upon you.

Each time I reflect on my life, tears of joy, thankfulness, and humility stream down my face. Despite the greatness I've experienced in every aspect of my life, I remain grounded, knowing that God can take as easily as He gives. I've witnessed numerous fresh starts, reminding me to remain humble and gentle, as Ephesians 4:2 teaches. Jesus is worth more than anything we fear losing, and in my journey, I've gained far more than I've lost, even in parting with people. I am grateful for closed doors, knowing that God replaces what was lost with blessings beyond measure. Trusting in God's plan means discerning between true blessings and deceptive gifts from the enemy. Not every blessing is from God, and I am careful not to accept what I haven't earned through hard work and righteousness.

Wisdom and knowledge

Satan's profound knowledge of God doesn't translate into love for Him. Understanding God intellectually doesn't necessarily mean having faith in Him. We are all God's children, but not everyone chooses to embrace that identity. To become a true child of God, one must accept Jesus/God into their hearts and rid themselves of hate, envy, and jealousy. Through God's grace, we can overcome these negative emotions.

Remember, the Spirit within you is greater than any worldly influence (1 John 4:4). Each new day is an opportunity to live life to the fullest, make a positive impact, and inspire others. Reflect on the significance of the cross, the nails, and the forgiveness it symbolizes. Through Christ, we are redeemed and given new life.

God continuously opens doors in my life without me even having to knock. Our relationship is solid, and He has the power to open doors without any drama attached. God is the author of my life story; He has been writing each chapter since the day I was born. He knows everything I've had to endure, and now He's ready for my story to be told and published, which is why you hold it in your hands.

What God has in store for me is far greater than anything I've experienced before. Faith means trusting God even when His plan isn't clear. The greatest test of faith is being able to thank the Lord even when we don't get what we want. I remember praying for things I have now and those yet to come.

Fight your battles with prayer; victory is assured. Everything happens at the right moment, so keep moving forward step by step. God wants to know He can trust you with His blessings. Many have received what they asked for and turned away from God; don't let that be you.

Patience equals discipline and wisdom. Everything you need is already within you; don't rely on others to ignite your passion. Stay focused, and something better than you ever imagined will come when you least expect it. God will always provide, even if it looks different from what you expected. Have faith, not just in the belief that God will act, but in the certainty that He will.

It's amazing to reflect on the journey with my guardian angels, who have been by my side through it all. The first one took on a challenging five-year contract a decade ago, and although the process may have burned him out, it made me stronger. I hope he's done with therapy by now! The second one was a bit easier due to the groundwork laid by the first, and I added the practice of meditation when God assigned her to me.

Now, the two angels currently assigned to me, after two years, are in a more relaxed state, patiently waiting for me to seek their help while diligently guarding me from the demons that lurk around daily. Initially, they faced a rough time keeping me safe amidst constant attacks. However, as we persevered together in spiritual warfare, God tested us to see if we could handle what lay ahead as a team, with me placing my trust in them as I do in Him. God has tasked them to watch over me every day, all day, stationed on my shoulders like silent sentinels. I can feel their presence as I type these words; they dance on my shoulders, providing constant encouragement while fulfilling their divine duty of shielding me from all evil and harm.

They affirm that the spiritual, mental, physical, and emotional work I've done and continue to do in my daily life deserves accolades. They assure me that I'm not only helping myself but also assisting others with life choices, and they urge me to persist in my endeavors. They confirm that the decisions I've made and those I'm making align perfectly with my soul's purpose and life mission and that my efforts are celebrated in heaven. They humorously mention that even the other angels want my autograph! Improving myself from the inside out is an ongoing process for as long as God allows me to remain on this Earth. We all fall short of God's glorious standards, but through His grace, He freely makes us right in His sight, as Romans 3:23-24 reminds us. When prayers stem from a genuine heart and are offered to others, God hears them and blesses them openly.

Heavenly Father,

With a humble and grateful heart, I come before You, asking for Your presence to manifest in the lives of all who have journeyed through our book and desire to know You intimately. May Your divine touch be felt by each reader, confirming Your reality and drawing them into a deeper relationship with You, just as You have blessed me. Grant them the same peace, joy, and happiness that You bestow upon me daily, regardless of the trials and tests they may face. Thank You for walking alongside us, never forsaking us, even in our moments of solitude. I acknowledge Your constant presence and ask that You continue to guide and support me, Your humble servant.

Thank You, Father, for Your attentive ear and Your actions on my behalf. In the name of Jesus, I offer this prayer, believing that You will fulfil it according to Your perfect will. From this path, I will not depart. Amen.

She extends a helping hand to the poor and opens her arms to the needy (Proverbs 31:20). I've experienced firsthand how God sends people to me, not just crossing paths but inviting them to know Him through me. Most don't realize who stands before them because they see me, but God gives me the words to speak to them.

Let me share a testimony: recently, while at work, God sent a lady to me because He knew what she was going through. He spoke to me, prompting her to hit her knees and start praying. It was an incredible experience that nearly overwhelmed me, but I know my power in Christ Jesus, and it humbled me more than ever before. She returned the next day, reluctant to leave my presence like the day before. All of this occurred in my office, where God's will reigns supreme. Nothing and no one can thwart it. I am compelled to operate in my gifts, remaining steadfast on this path. It's for eagles, not birds. God blesses me to bless others, and I've witnessed His blessings manifest in various ways. I've learned that it's not just about me; I have a life mission to fulfil. I pray that the Lord continues to pour down blessings upon me so that I may pour them out onto others, just as He has with this life-changing book. God knew the world needed it. Now, it's time to apply its wisdom to your life!

GOD IS LOVE, and countless broken individuals in this world need Him. Their demons overpower them, leading to the existence of evil and wickedness, but this will soon be no more, in Jesus' name.

Don't let your loneliness lower your standards. The truth is, you won't fit in with everyone. But the good news is, the great ones never do. I've never fit in, never wanted to. I do my own thing. Listen and silent are spelt with the same letters. A seed grows with no sound, but a tree falls with a huge noise. Destruction also has noise, but creation is quiet. This is the power of silence. Grow silently. You are an incredibly powerful being and have the ability to heal yourself by truly believing in it. This is not wishful thinking; this is a documented fact.

Set some goals, stay quiet about them, smash them, and then clap for yourself! I've learned to make fewer announcements and more moves and to appreciate all the little wins in my everyday life. We often become so caught up in the stress of our jobs and our social lives that we forget to thank God for the little blessings He gives us each day. Pause and reflect on your blessings over the past week, no matter how small they might have been, and notice how God will reward you with many more in the days to come.

Gone are the days when all we can do is please people. As we mature, we become more careful. Not everyone needs to know your whereabouts and your next steps. You'll never hear a tree making noise when it grows. Grow silently, bloom quietly. Making moves in silence gives people less opportunity to pray against you.

You must learn a new way of thinking before you master a new way to be. Don't be a prisoner of your past. It was a lesson, not a life sentence. If you want to fly, you have to let go of the things that weigh you down. I had to learn that myself! Miracles start to happen when you give as much energy to your dream as you do to your fears. A future, a vibrant future without God/Jesus, doesn't exist. Whenever you feel crushed in the spirit, under pressure, pressed, or in darkness by your thoughts, you're in a powerful place of transformation. Trust the process.

People will judge you because you keep starting over, so what? Live like you're about to enter the best chapter of your life. May the new chapter in your life be better than your last one? If there is no struggle, there is no progress. I'm clapping for you because you never gave up. It's easy to judge; it's more difficult to understand. Understanding requires compassion, patience, and a willingness to believe that good hearts sometimes choose poor methods. Through judging, we separate; through understanding, we grow. The one who judges never starts anything; that's why they have a lot of time on their hands to watch what you are doing.

I've learned not to tell anyone what I'm doing until it's done. Outside energy can throw off goals! Allowing people to be wrong about you or a situation while keeping your peace and focus is the most misunderstood power move you will ever make. People look so different when you don't care what they think about you anymore. Surround yourself with those who are on the same mission as you. You bless or curse your days with the things you say. The words you speak become the house you live in. Let your words bless your life daily.

I'm in a chapter in my life where God has given me the power, strength, and happiness that comes with a peace that is unexplainable. If you have not experienced it for yourself, you know nothing of the peace I am talking about. Find out for yourself. I decree and declare I will spend the rest of my life laughing, being happy, and loved. I will spend the rest of my life on Earth:

- Embracing happiness and joy, regardless of external circumstances.
- Refusing to allow negative energy to infiltrate my positive space, surrounding myself only with those who bring joy and growth into my life.
- Walking the road of life with God by my side every step of the way, acknowledging that I can't do it without Him.
- Pursuing my goals with determination and faith, knowing that God's plans for me cannot be thwarted.

- Mastering the art of lifting others up by speaking the truth with love and compassion.
- Embracing setbacks as opportunities for comebacks, knowing that nothing can ultimately stop me.
- Moving in silence, being productive, and letting my actions speak louder than words.
- Embracing creativity and authenticity, being unapologetically myself.
- Always remember that God is above me to bless me, before me to guide me, behind me to protect me, beside me to comfort me, and inside me to sustain me.
- Trusting in God's divine timing to remind the world of His power and glory.

One minute after a believer dies:

- Angels usher your soul to heaven.
- You immediately enter God's presence.
- You are conscious and in command of your thinking, feeling, speech, and memories.
- You participate in magnificent worship with angels and believers before the throne of God and Christ.
- You are aware to some degree of activities and events on Earth.
- You recognize and communicate with believers who preceded you to heaven.

I can't fathom the fate of a non-believer. Dear reader, heed the call to embrace God while you still can. The concept of normalcy is shifting; Jesus is our constant. (Honestly), are you ready to stand before God/Jesus? The devil strives to deter you, but our faith must prevail. While many celebrate the moon landing as humanity's peak, my friends, the true pinnacle was Jesus emerging from the tomb!

Me now! I'm evolving into a confident woman, fortified by faith and devoid of fear.

- I'm pursuing my childhood dreams by writing this remarkable book, anticipating the myriad opportunities it will unveil.
- I'm advancing my education to become a licensed nail technician. As I type, I'm halfway through school. By the book's release, I'll have completed my journey.
- Contemplating launching my own t-shirt business, with plans already underway by the time you hold this book.
- Exploring the possibility of ghostwriting for others, aligning my aspirations with God's will.

As I conclude this book, I embark on a week-long fast during Holy Week 2023 until Passover's end. The hand of God has graced me and my children abundantly. Blessings have poured forth to the extent that my daughter remarked, "Mom, I'm not sure what we've done, but we're being rewarded." I replied, *"Prayer is potent, baby"*.

Your life can undergo remarkable transformations within a year. You must love yourself enough to demand more and have the courage and discipline to pursue it. At the appointed time, the Lord will make it happen (Isaiah 60:22). Nothing can deter me! I've undergone significant inner growth to protect my energy. No one can diminish my vibrancy. I remain steadfast in my aura. Few things rival the power of a beautiful, focused woman unswayed by distractions. Watch out, future, here I come, in the mighty name of Jesus.

I serve a God with a divine plan for my life, greater than any challenge. My mission is to immerse myself in love, leaving no space for hate, regret, worry, or fear. The greatest lesson I've learned is to keep my plans and dreams guarded. Every encounter sees me thriving more than before. Don't abandon your aspirations; waiting is tough, but regret is tougher. Knowing oneself means deciding whom to shed from your life. I'm content staying in, relishing the peace and joy of solitude. It's fine to socialize, but I prefer avoiding negativity and odd company. I prioritize my peace unfailingly.

At this moment, I pursue my dreams with unwavering determination. Nothing can deter me. I'm defying expectations by penning this transformative book and becoming a licensed nail technician simultaneously. I am destined to be a bestselling author, fulfilling a prophecy whispered by God years ago. Despite facing adversities, I persisted, emerging stronger each time. Most individuals I've encountered were like monsters, harboring toxic intentions, except for my beloved cousin, who always cheered me on. Sometimes, true character is revealed when you're not looking. People often overlook the profound value of genuine care from another. Having overcome my inner demons, I now bask in an indescribable peace and joy— God-given gifts that fortify my spirit. I am fully aware of my identity and worth, a treasure many will seek endlessly. Blessings upon those who discover what I have found.

For years, I shielded others by withholding my truth, inadvertently losing myself in the process. My happiness waned, drained by the darkness surrounding me. Yet, upon reclaiming my essence, everything shifted in my favor. Now, healed and liberated from toxicity and narcissism, I radiate the light God intended for me. While those who sought to break me remain fractured, I stand whole and vibrant. It's common to be disliked when others haven't heard your side of the story. Choosing silence to maintain peace can be a trauma response, disregarding our own boundaries. Regardless, I vow to occupy space and wield my voice. Trusting in God's plan has brought me immeasurable blessings, a testament to His power.

My goal moving forward is to craft a future devoid of recovery—a life lived fully in the present, leaving the past behind. Setting boundaries is essential, even if it means embracing anti-social behavior in a world of conformity. My mantra remains unwavering as I pursue my ambitions: I will triumph, not immediately, but inevitably. In times of hardship, I find solace in God's presence, knowing He equips me for any challenge. Always be prepared, for God's blessings are boundless, and the return of Jesus is unknown (Matthew 24:44).

In 2023 and 2024, I refuse to be pressed, pregnant, bothered or broke. Instead, I'll be found inspiring others, continuously evolving, evading negativity, and conquering my goals and dreams with unwavering determination. In the hustle of life, I'm too engrossed in productivity, savoring the sweetness of success, and chasing my dreams to dwell on anything else. My current aspiration is to lead a soft life devoid of anger, unforgiveness, and resentment, as these emotions breed struggle, sickness, and hatred. Instead, I crave love, positivity, a pure heart, and tranquility—all gifts bestowed upon me by the Almighty God, in Jesus' name.

My lifestyle prioritizes health—both physical and spiritual. My heart is aligned with God, my energy radiates positivity, and my soul is bathed in light. My sole ambition is to please God, for I am destined for greatness not by my design but by His divine plan for me. The contents of my heart shape my destiny, and my determination shapes my journey.

May my words inspire benevolent deeds in the name of Jesus. True success lies not in personal achievements but in the inspiration we instill in others. I harbor goals so monumental that revealing them to small-minded individuals feels uncomfortable. My greatest strength lies in the privacy I maintain. Privacy, to me, is synonymous with peace—a luxury I safeguard fiercely. As I age, I grow quieter, realizing the folly of wasting time on trivial matters. I observe keenly, understanding that silence often speaks volumes. I am deserving of the success I've toiled for and the blessings that await me. Regardless of my wealth, I vow to remain humble, continuing to give selflessly. Humility, to me, means recognizing that our purpose on Earth is not to amass importance but to make a difference in the lives of others. I place my trust in God, knowing He will provide and protect me, just as He has done throughout my life.

Why would He stop now?

This question fuels my pursuits, even when they seem insurmountable. I firmly believe in the power of manifestation—I can attract anything I desire. Relaxation is key in this process; there's no need to beg or stress. I stand firm in my belief that what I want will come to me effortlessly.

This chapter of my life is about making room for more blessings. My relationship with God is unshakeable, and His faithfulness has never wavered. In this phase, I embody qualities that reflect both calmness and readiness, humility and confidence. God has instilled in me bold courage for such a time as this, guiding my decisions and freeing me from fear. Today, there is much to smile about:

- I am filled with the Father, the Son, and the Holy Spirit.
- I am liberated from toxic relationships.
- I have severed all soul ties.
- I understand my identity and the power I possess in Christ Jesus.

I refuse to diminish my dreams to fit my current reality; instead, I focus on upgrading my attitude, discipline, and skills to align with my destiny. I walk confidently, knowing that part of life's journey is discovering and embracing my uniqueness. As I do the inner work, my life is continuously upgraded.

Being authentic in a world of conformity is a remarkable achievement. I choose to shift my focus to the positive and embrace the amazing aspects of my life. I celebrate the present moment, expressing gratitude for those in my life and for those who have departed. My miracle is intertwined with my gratitude, and I eagerly anticipate the abundance that awaits. I am enough. Filled with sparkle and compassion, I strive to make the world a better place. Love, kindness, and loyalty define my character. I embrace truth, adventure, and support. As a woman, I am more than sufficient.

Happiness is an inside job—I refuse to assign anyone else the power over my life. It's my responsibility to create happiness every day. I choose love, joy, and freedom. Life may present challenges, but I choose to remain flexible and grateful. People may bring difficulty, but I choose freedom. No dream is too big or too small. I raise my standards and pursue my deepest desires, knowing that God will meet me there. I am transformed spiritually, physically, mentally, emotionally, and financially. Abundance and prosperity are my birthright, and I am committed to manifesting miracles. Though some days may seem uncertain, I press forward with determination. I am leveling up, surpassing my previous self. Manifestations may take time, but I trust that they are coming. I continue to smash barriers, understanding that the cost of regret far outweighs the possibility of failure.

Attitude reality check

Attitude is indeed a powerful force that shapes our lives. When our attitude is positive and electric, we thrive and manifest greatness. Our attitude reflects our inner state, influencing our interactions and outcomes. Simple acts of kindness can have a profound impact on those silently struggling around us.

Turning *"can't"* into *"can"* and dreams into plans is a testament to our resilience and determination. I find peace in knowing that what is meant for me will never truly be lost. Some days, I embody the strength of a lioness, unapologetically owning who I am while following the path set by the Lamb. Being at peace means no longer seeking validation from others or feeling the need to prove ourselves. Guarding our peace becomes paramount, knowing its worth exceeds any need for validation or vindication.

The true riches lie in wisdom, the strongest weapon in prayer and patience, and the best security in faith in God/Jesus. Laughter and happiness serve as the strongest tonic against life's challenges. Consider the preciousness of a soul sought after by both God and the devil. The anointing within us drives the enemy crazy. Armed with the Holy Spirit, our armor is impenetrable, allowing us to withstand any challenge. In all aspects of life, courage is required to stretch our limits, express our power, and fulfill our potential. Education and growth transform us into smart, solid, and healing individuals, not merely defined by outward appearance.

Balance is key—neither letting success inflate our ego nor allowing failure to deflate our spirit. True leadership lies in caring for others' development rather than exploiting them for personal gain. For those with good hearts and intentions, know that every action is recorded, and God watches over and loves us unconditionally. Trust in His love and protection as we navigate life's journey.

Indeed, God's patience and slow anger are boundless, even for those who walk in darkness. His love and forgiveness are available to all who repent and turn from their wicked ways. No one can hide their brokenness from God, for He sees all and loves us unconditionally. In these tumultuous times, where the world seems to be descending into chaos, turning to God is essential for survival. Preparedness is crucial as we navigate through the challenges of these last days, with biblical prophecies unfolding before our eyes. The peace that surpasses all understanding is found in God through Christ Jesus. In times of uncertainty and fear, His presence in our hearts and minds brings comfort and assurance.

"Fear not," says the Lord. He watches over us, guiding us through every trial and tribulation. As we keep our eyes on Him and trust in His divine plan, we find strength and courage to face whatever lies ahead.

Chapter 16:
Lesson Learned

Lesson One: There will always be those who feel you don't deserve what you have.

Lesson Two: Forget them; their opinions don't matter.

Lesson Three: Stop giving your energy to unnecessary things.

Regardless of our backgrounds, appearances, or circumstances, each of us possesses invaluable gifts within—strength, beauty, courage, and more. While these gifts may not be tangible, they have the power to enrich our lives and help us overcome challenges. Reflecting on past experiences, I realize that every rejection has redirected me towards something beautiful. It was all about sharing my story, a narrative crafted by God since my birth, to inspire others to overcome their own challenges. While we can't change the past, we can learn from it and forgive ourselves. Today is the perfect moment to begin anew, as nothing in our past can prevent God's love for us.

Loving yourself

Remember, people may come and go, but you'll always be with yourself. Maintain positive thoughts, care for your body, and treat yourself with respect and gentleness. Above all, love yourself. Your path is yours alone, so do what's best for you—no one else can walk in your shoes.

Challenging yourself

When negative thoughts arise, counteract them with three positive ones. Confront the monster of negativity with the power of positivity. Train yourself to switch gears and focus on the bright side—it's a skill worth mastering!

Getting started

Stop making excuses and start taking action. Begin where you are, with what you have. It's tempting to wait for the perfect moment or gather more resources, but greatness starts with a single step. Get started now, and watch your resources grow along the way. Don't waste another minute doubting yourself—dive into what you truly want to achieve.

Moving forward

Face your fears head-on. Avoiding scary situations only gives them power over you. Take that first step, no matter how small, and keep moving forward. You'll be amazed at how much better you feel once you confront your fears.

You can do this

Stay on track by avoiding distractions and investing your time and energy into productivity. Keep your goals in sight at all times. Stay focused, determined, and humble. It's amazing how your mind works when you're focused on greatness. Take action on your thoughts, like starting a life coaching class, and trust that God will open doors for you. Boom, boom!

You are never too late

It's never too late to embark on your journey towards your dreams. You deserve a happy, wonderful, and joyful life. Set goals and work diligently to achieve them. You have all the necessary resources within you to make it happen in your own unique way. I believe in you, the reader.

What do you have to lose? Honestly, what do you have to gain? Honestly. Just like Solomon asked for wisdom and God added wealth, and Abraham asked for a son and God gave him generations, may God give you more than you ask for. In Jesus' name, Amen! You're going to make it. You're not just going to barely crawl into your next season; you're going to rise and run into it with a smile on your face and a heart full of grace.

It's all about you

The world is constantly spinning; this is your chance to make your life all about you. Start thinking about what you want and put things into place to achieve anything you put your mind to. There is no better time than now!

Affirm:

- I am living in abundance.
- I am wealthy.
- I am successful.
- I am loved.
- I am at peace.

You have to claim and believe it to be true to receive it. Nothing to be stressed about. It's easier said than done to stop stressing over things we cannot control. However, this is a vital step in moving forward and trusting God. The sooner you realize it is out of your control, the sooner you will feel more content, confident, and at peace about any situation you are in.

Manifesting what you want. You have the power to decree and declare anything in your life. This is your opportunity to stand in your power and do it. God knows your intentions and desires. He will deliver in His divine timing and in His holy way. Believe in yourself. Love yourself enough to preserve your power for the people and situations that are worth it.

Declaration

Decree and declare: From this point on, you will put yourself in better situations that leave you excited, breathless, happy, smiling with gratitude, and abundant. If you have read this far, it is time for you to let God know that you are ready to receive all that He has for you, and you will do right by the miracles He bestows onto you.

I've learned from experience that you grow differently when you have good people with good intentions in your life, and confidence comes from the promises you make to yourself. Confidence makes you better. You are the most important person in your life. You always were and always will be. You are the only person who is going to stick around within your lifetime. Take care of yourself. Always have a unique character like salt; its presence is not felt, but its absence makes everything tasteless.

Repeat: Today, I will do what others won't, so tomorrow, I can do what others can't. I've learned that you free yourself when you learn to accept yourself as you are, flaws and all. Nothing holds you back more than your own insecurities. All of us have this choice:

- To do... or not to do.
- To be... or not to be.
- To be all... or to be less.

- Or even to be nothing at all.

When the mind is weak, the situation is a problem. When the mind is balanced, the situation is challenged. When the mind is strong, the situation becomes an opportunity.

Motivation

Sometimes, people have the habit of blaming others for their misfortunes instead of themselves. Be the change. Make the difference you need in your own life to be happy and, most of all, successful. Know who you are. Know what you want. Know what you deserve. Say yes to new opportunities. Take this as a chance to grow. If it doesn't feel right, say no!

Start your day off

I've also learned to work hard in silence and let my success be my noise. If it makes you happy, do it anyway. Whether or not it makes sense, whether or not you are sure about it, and whether or not you are good at it. Don't think about what can happen in a month or in a year. Just focus on the 24 hours in front of you and do what you can to get closer to where you want to be. Wake up every morning and tell yourself you want a wonderful day full of goodness. Once you start to believe in what you deserve, you will be amazed at what you begin to attract. I expect good things to come to me every day, and they do because I expect it.

Growth

First comes the comfort zone, where you feel safe and in control. Next comes the fear zone, where you may find yourself making excuses and lacking self-confidence.

Then comes the learning zone, where you acquire new skills, face challenges, solve problems, and outgrow your comfort zone. Finally, the growth zone comes upon you, where you have found your purpose in life and your life's mission. You are now conquering objectives, accomplishing and setting new goals while living out your dreams.

Freedom

You are free to breathe and rest, whether or not you feel like everything is in place. No matter how heavy life's moments may feel, there will be boundless peace and positivity waiting for you. Rest well, knowing tomorrow is coming and you have another chance at making something of yourself. Until then, rest, my brothers and sisters in Christ.

Exploration

Something new means a fresh opportunity to shed any old values or traditions that are holding you back and explore what's out there. There are so many new and exciting things for you to try. Why are you holding back? Go be successful.

Knowledge

Knowledge isn't just about what we know; it's also about our capacity to learn new things and how swiftly we can do so. This ability to learn, which can be cultivated and refined, is just as crucial as the knowledge we already possess. When you emit positive vibrations, you'll be astonished by what comes back to you. Positivity always prevails!

Being Thankful

Expressing gratitude can truly transform your life. An attitude of thankfulness can improve relationships, work environments, family dynamics, and overall satisfaction. It's not a challenging feat to achieve; you need to shift your perspective on life. Like any worthwhile endeavor, practicing gratitude needs to become a habit. Being mindful of everything in your life helps you make better decisions and create the life you want to live.

Dear Father God,

I come to You with gratitude overflowing for guiding me through this transformative journey of writing. Your presence has been my strength, carrying me through each step and shaping this book into what it is meant to be. I trust in Your divine plan for this manuscript and eagerly anticipate the wonders You will work through.

This book, a testament to Your grace and my perseverance, is dedicated solely to You, Father. Without Your hand upon me, I could not have ventured into this breakthrough healing journey. Every word penned, every page turned, has been imbued with Your wisdom and love.

Thank You, Father, for entrusting me with this task. It is an honor beyond measure to be chosen as Your vessel for spreading Your message of hope and redemption. In Jesus' name, I offer this work to You, knowing that Your will guides its path.

Dear Heavenly Father,

As I reach the conclusion of this remarkable journey, I am compelled to come before You in gratitude. Thank You for guiding me through the profound transformations I've experienced while crafting this life-changing book.

In the depths of writing, I've encountered invaluable lessons in life, undergoing spiritual, mental, and emotional breakthroughs that have shaped me profoundly. I am grateful for the diverse array of characters who have crossed my path—both those who have illuminated my journey and those who have challenged me. Each one has contributed to the richness of my experience.

Above all, I am indebted to You for Your unwavering love and boundless forgiveness. Your presence has been the driving force behind every word penned, every revelation unearthed. I am humbled by the miracles that continue to unfold in my life, evidence of Your omnipotent grace.

As I offer this book into Your hands, I do so with anticipation and trust, knowing that Your divine plan will unfold in ways far beyond my comprehension. Thank You for the countless blessings You have bestowed upon me, and thank You in advance for the wonders You will work through this manuscript.

Your Humbled Daughter,

L. SPIKES
The Chosen One

www.ingramcontent.com/pod-product-compliance
Lightning Source LLC
Chambersburg PA
CBHW071328120626

46546CB00002B/488